COSMOLOGY
OF THE SELF

Shaykh Fadhlalla Haeri

Zahra Publications

ISBN: 978-0-958417-65-5
eISBN: 978-1-928329-22-0
Published by Zahra Publications
Distributed and Published by Zahra Publications
PO Box 50764
Wierda Park 0149 Centurion
South Africa
www.zahrapublications.pub
www.zahrapublications.com

Cover artwork has been adjusted; original artwork by JAKOBHANSSON
https://www.deviantart.com/jakobhansson/art/The-Duality-Tree-189122452
Designed and typeset in South Africa by Quintessence Publishing
Cover Design by Quintessence Publishing
Project Management by Quintessence Publishing

Table of Contents

Book Description vii
About the Author ix
Preface xi

Chapter 1: Where Heaven and Earth Meet 1
The Unknown 1
The Divine Spark of the Spirit *(Ruh)* 2
The Heart 3
The Original Blueprint *(Fitra)* 4
From the Fitra to the Perfect Man 5
From the Unity of Essence to the Unity of Actions 7
Shari`a, Tariqa, Haqiqa 9
Chapter 2: The Self (Nafs) 13
The *Nafs* (Self) in the Qur'an 13
The Forms the *Nafs* Takes 18
Grooming the *Nafs* 20
`Aql (Faculty of Reason) and *Qalb* (the Heart) 26

Chapter 3: The Ways of the Heart 31
The Inner Heart – *Fu'ad* and *Lubb* 32
The Heart, Man and His Spirit 34
The Monitoring Self – *Raqib* 35
The Recording Companion – *Qarin* 36
Insight *(Basira)*, Gnosis *(Ma`rifa)* and Unveiling *(Kashf)* ... 37
Gnosis – *Ma`rifa* 39

Chapter 4: The Four Facets of the Bondsman 43
The Bondsman *(`Abd)* of Allah 44
Rububiyya 45

Loyalty *(Birr)* 50

Ruhaniyya 51

Insaniyya 55

The First Man – Adam 56

Mankind 57

`*Ubudiyya* 58

From *Rabb* to `*Abd* 61

Action and Transformation 62

The Bondsman in the Arena of Action (`*Amal*) 63

Salat – Prayer 65

The Path to Knowledge 65

Conclusion **69**

A Glossary of Key Terms **71**

Appendix **79**

Notes on Diagrams 79

Book Description

For the serious seeker of Reality, the way to this transcendent knowledge has been clearly indicated by the Prophet: "Whoever knows himself, knows his Lord". Coming to know the inner landscape of the human self is one of the essential foundations for progress on the path of knowledge.

This book is a practical and accessible distillation of the *tawhidi* (unitive) Islamic teachings and insights into the map of the human self. Shaykh Fadhlalla Haeri has sought to furnish the reader with the fundamental elements and insights into the make-up of the individual self and how the various elements of spirituality and humanity interact within us.

About the Author

Shaykh Fadhlalla Haeri was born in Karbala, Iraq, a descendant of several generations of well-known and revered spiritual leaders. Educated in Europe and America, he founded a number of companies in the Middle East and worked as a consultant in the oil industry.

He travelled extensively on a spiritual quest which led to his eventual rediscovery of the pure and original Islamic heritage of his birth.

In 1980 he established the Zahra Trust, a charitable organization with centers in the USA, Britain and the Middle East, which makes traditional Islamic teachings more widely available through courses and publications, promotes the revival of traditional systems of healing and supports a variety of charitable programs.

Shaykh Fadhlalla is currently engaged in lecturing and writing books and commentaries on the Holy Qur'an and related subjects, with particular emphasis on ethics, self-development and gnosis (`irfan).

In 2004, he established the Academy of Self Knowledge, http://www.askonline.co.za, which offers teachings on self knowledge and the Prophetic revealed path.

Preface

This book was drawn from a series of talks given by Shaykh Fadhlalla Haeri at a gathering in Sweden. The name of our location, was Hjartered, meaning heart's ease. For those of us that were there, the gathering was a cool drink of the sweetest water, amidst the beauty of the forests and lakes, which touched our hearts and inspired us.

I: Where Heaven and Earth Meet

The Unknown

Creation is rooted in the mysterious. It includes the worlds of the spirits, the angels, the jinn, and myriad aspects of the spiritual realm. God describes those of us who accept this as true as 'the ones who believe in the unseen' (Qur'an 2:3). Just as the child needs to be told to groom itself, to wash its hands and tidy its room, we too, have to be constantly reminded of the vast, unfathomable unseen worlds that are far greater than our seen world.

From the unseen world of *haqiqa*, or Reality, Allah reminds us: 'I was a Hidden Treasure and I loved to be known, so I created.' The basis of creation is love. Its purpose is to know the foundation and essence of life, which is why we all love to know with absolute certitude. The mind will drive us on until we come to be sure. We are programmed to know.

Everything hinges on *tawhid*, unity. What we see as creation is a unified field that rests upon an unstructured, invisible foundation not subject to time and space as we know it. Human beings are the 'middle people'; the interspace between what seems tangible and what is beyond. All systems of knowledge, all the true prophets and teachers, and every true religion acknowledge this; one aspect of us relates to existential realities on earth, which are to do with cause and effect, while another keeps us attuned to our origins before time. Being on what is called 'the path' teaches alertness and discrimination.

We are here to interact and deal with nature, with the world and its inhabitants, in a way that is best for us. If we do not want this, then we become escapists. If we do then we should know that we have access to more than just the material world that we see around us. A glimpse of this other realm of non-existence is obtained during sleep and that is why we love deep sleep – because we need to recharge ourselves and enhance that part of us which is beyond words.

The Divine Spark of the Spirit (*Ruh*)

There is within us a Divine spark that has no limitations. This is the *ruh*. Its origins lie in the realm of non-time and non-space. We yearn for infinite space, for endless stretches of land, seas, and vast oceans whose horizons are invisible; we long for peace and tranquility. It is that same zone within us that contains pre-existence, post-existence, as well as pre-cognition and post-cognition. Death demonstrates the point at which we will return material borrowed from the earth. We will continue to carry an aspect of ourselves into the timeless, space less zone after death, which will be the reverse of the way in which it manifests here. At death and beyond the body will not contain the *ruh* but rather the *ruh* will be imprinted with the image of the body. As we progress along the path of enlightenment, we know this as a fact rather than merely believe in it as a theory.

While the importance of rationality in this world of duality and opposites is undeniable, the *ruh* transcends the limits of reasoning. Since such knowledge is based on *tawhid*, it is not subject to dialectical reasoning. God says in the Qur'an: 'They ask you about the spirit – say: "It is from the command of my

Lord'" (Qur'an: 17:85), meaning it is from the unseen. Its nature is unknown.

The Heart

If the heart can be well enough to send us the right signals, the attainment of clarity of vision and an unfailing ability to discriminate between what is harmful and what is of benefit becomes easy. No one can judge another's heart, which can change; we can only hold each other accountable for our outer actions. However, the heart may become deadened to its spiritual reality, as a result of the thick layers of 'rust' we allow it to accumulate. At this stage it may not be possible to cure it of its ills; we cannot even chisel the rust off any more.

Many of us, however, need to make use of the chisel that Allah provides for us through hardship, illness and sometimes abrupt changes in our existential situation. Our nature is to immediately ask 'why? – why have I lost my job? why has my husband left me?' – when shaken up in such a way. If we take it on trust that God has based His creation on mercy and love, then from our wondering 'why' will come the light of knowledge. With the aid of this light, it becomes clear that perhaps we were drowning in emotionalism and are now paying a price for it. Perhaps we were seeking results which would have been harmful and had too many expectations. We may have been reacting when we are meant to act.

Everyone wants results and if our objectives are real, necessary and within the framework of our existential reality, God will honor the seeker. If, on the other hand, the aim is to embellish our outer surroundings or forms, then our objectives are frivolous. The tailor may succeed in giving us a good image with an exquisitely tailored suit, but of what use is this to us if we remain misshapen and ugly inside? We all love perfection and even wanting to have a pleasing outer aspect is a facet of loving the Perfect Designer. However, our love of perfection need not mean fixed physical perfection. There is only disappointment if we stop short at the physical. This happens because no sooner do we place a certain value on anything that is sensory, at the expense of its meaning and ultimately its essence, than it decays and disappears. This is its natural reality.

The cosmic Big Bang that originated creation echoes the shock of awakening in the rise of human consciousness. We have come from non-existence and we will return to our origin. Just as there will be a collapse of the planetary cosmos, so will there be a collapse of our physical cosmos, our bodies. Indeed, the Qur'an speaks of two deaths, two events of importance for us. One is the individual end of this world – my individual world ends when I die – and the other, when the cosmic world ceases to be.

The Original Blueprint *(Fitra)*

Time is in motion and yet something within us yearns for a certainty that is before time and beyond time. We desire outer harmony in order to grasp its meaning within the original blueprint that is inherent in every created thing. This primal blueprint is called *fitra* in Arabic. The Prophet said: 'Every child is created with an intact *fitra* and is born in a state of submission, *(Islam)*'. He goes on to say, 'but it is the parents, culture, and society that make it a Christian, a Jew, or a fire-worshipper.' Environmental and other external influences modify the blueprint. This brings about an altered output. The original Divine Imprint with which each child is born has been tampered with.

One rather inadequate word that alludes to this blueprint is 'conscience'. *Fitra*, however, is a more precise, neutral term which also means, amongst other things, 'the original crack' that brings about creation. We shall call it 'the original self.'

From the *Fitra* to the Perfect Man

The discovery of our *fitra* plays a key role in the transformation and illumination of the soul. The *fitra* has come about as a result of a divine gift and encapsulates the complementary male/female principles. After four months the fetus in the womb has *ruh*, after which it develops a *nafs*. The *fitra* arises from what will become the *ruh*. So that original blueprint, the *fitra*, contains within it the entire plan of the *self*. While the lower aspects of this *self*, the human and animal aspects, pertain to the earth, the higher, spiritual aspects link us to what is beyond time/space.

This is the domain of `*alam al-ghayb*, the unseen world – the world of the angelic forces – which exerts considerable influence on us without our being fully aware of it. We have evidence of the existence of such forces by our crude interventions in physics, harnessing some of these powers without quite understanding the essence of the laws to which they are subject, electricity being just one example. The worlds these forces inhabit seem to overlap ours; their lowest zone being at the edge of our highest. References to space/time are a reflection of the limitations of language and are only an aid to understanding a reality beyond our comprehension.

A few decades ago we were less able to harness some of these energies in existence. Now, for example, we have a clearer understanding of the nature of many physical realities. We know that light travels in certain wave patterns and that it is formed in bundles of discrete quantities. Visible light is of only a limited spectrum, from red to violet. Beyond infra-red and ultraviolet, light moves into other wave forms that are invisible. The world of the *arwah* – (spirits or souls, plural of *ruh*) and its relationship to the original self is the same as the relationship between the total spectrum of light and visible light: we can only speak of the aspect of light that is visible – the soul.

A part of man contains the world of spirit, *ruh*, which is *ruhaniyya*, while another part relates to the human world, called *insaniyya*.

During its journey through time and space, the original self develops into a persona, the so-called 'you' and 'I'. If we aim to attain the higher values as shown and lived by our prophets, then *ruhaniyya*, the spiritual side of our nature, is developed. If, however, the higher is neglected, then the lower self is reinforced.

This is not a denunciation of our life on earth. We are a microcosm of all that is in existence; mineral, vegetable and animal, as well as our own unique human qualities. If all this is taken care of and given its due, then the original self will drive man towards the state of *insan al-kamil*, the complete or perfect man, denying neither spirituality nor humanity, and who is served by the angels.

There is a zone of the unknown, which we have named 'Heaven'. This zone interacts with its inferior and opposite, which we call 'Earth'. Where 'Heaven' meets 'Earth' or the *ruh* connects with matter, there arises this fusion in the field between them, which we defined earlier as the 'original self'.

We may see how essentially unified the nature of the original self is by looking at references from the Qur'an and the prophetic teachings. Allah says: 'I created you from one self' (Qur'an 4:1). This means that there is one original design, one blueprint, one *fitra*. From this blueprint is developed the form of the individual self, which is the so-called 'you'.

While each individual appears to be different from the other, this essential self is the foundation of each person's reality. Our forms are different: men and women. This difference is essential, as man without woman cannot embark on the journey of life and woman without man is equally only half the story. Even on a wider social scale, we need to complement each other as nations. God tells us in the Qur'an that He created us as different tribes and different nations so that we may interact and come to know and learn from each other. By acknowledging outer differences amongst people, the deeper realization is that we are the same in essence; that we are all seeking harmony, the aspect in us that never changes, that is always tranquil, and the source of divine reassurance. Allah is always there: 'I answer the call of the caller if he calls Me' (Qur'an 2:186).

From the Unity of Essence to the Unity of Actions

Creation began from the eternal void, which is referred to 'as the darkness of non-existence'. From this non-existence arise God's Divine Attributes (*al-sifat*) as symbolized by the ninety-nine 'most beautiful Names of Allah' (*al-asma' al-husna*), and

His words. God says: 'If you take all the woods in the world to make pens and take all the oceans as ink, seven times over, My words will not be completed' (Qur'an 31:27).

All of creation, with its myriad forces and dynamism, points us towards the knowledge of God, so that we know why we are here and who we are. Manifested creations are the Divine Actions (*al-af'al*). These connect and relate to each other through a unifying force both known and unknown. The study of cause and effect, logic and other sciences are attempts to discover the unifying factors behind creational actions.

Actions and Attributes are from one Essence (*dhat*) which we cannot describe. All we know is that it is the source from which everything emanates.

As travelers to higher knowledge, the first requisite is to contemplate and understand ourselves in *tawhid al-af'al*, the unity of action in crea-tion. We shall discover how actions relate with one another; how cause and effect link; how correct actions result in appropriate reactions, and so on. This is seeing the One behind the apparent 'two-ness' or duality of creation as an experiential reality and not just as a mystical quest. It is what drives us to want to know why we are unwell or unhappy. Once we come to know the connection we are relieved because it enables us to unify diverse aspects of our world.

When we see that all of creation links up within a unified field, then we recognize *tawhid al-sifat*, the unity of Attributes. To demonstrate this let us take the example of a man who wishes to project an image of piety. He even lies and cheats to maintain a good reputation. This apparent contradiction in his actions may puzzle us. The man, however, is being true to his objective of maintaining his image and is therefore willing to go to any lengths to achieve this. He is concerned with appearance and not with reality so he is connecting and unifying with the image. Unless we first awaken to *tawhid al-af'al*, we find difficulty in seeing *tawhid al-sifat*. We can easily see that the attributes of Mercy, Generosity and Power are linked. So are the others.

Awareness of the unity of Essence, *tawhid al-dhat*, becomes spontaneous as a result of our awakening to the unity of Action and Attributes. We are conscious of the diversity in creation but at the same time are aware that all of these differences lead back to the One Essence. That is when we can truly say *la ilaha illa'llah*, that there is no reality other than God Alone; that He is the Doer and He is the Creator of all. Our intellects and experience fail us because of the veil of reasoning, but the truth of our hearts and faith will confirm it.

Shari'A, Tariqa, Haqiqa

We have seen how the *ruh* energizes the self to produce a 'person'. The person contains the original self, the human *fitra*, and the divine spark. First the human aspect is dealt with; for example, hunger. Then the sublime part of the self develops and matures with the aid of discipline and awareness. The person's will, patience, faith, commitment and honesty are all vital. The seeker on the path of self-transformation and awakening is like a zoo-keeper: he recognizes all the wild animals within the self, but confines them to their cages and is safe from their wildness! The design of the original self, the *fitra*, contains *shari'a* and *haqiqa*; that is, the natural laws and the ultimate truth. We can also see how the original self can develop positively, remain under-developed, or become warped beyond the possibility of cure. We need to open our hearts to the divine light within and follow the natural laws as revealed by the Prophet.

To begin with one is concerned with oneself, and then we strive to improve the condition of our hearts. None of this however can be done in isolation. Real transformation and spiritual evolution occurs whilst serving others along the path. The overall cosmic drama has to be enacted constantly: microcosm and macrocosm; "I" and the world. One is the mirror image of the other.

The inner, microcosmic being needs to be groomed along the *tariqa* (path) and its 'prescription' which is the middle path. The *tariqa* offers the discipline of balance in a holistic way, in the *din* (the religion or life-transaction). It encourages diligence and commitment to the prescribed remedies, which are key elements in harnessing our lower, human *nafs* and enabling the higher to unfold. On the *tariqa* there must be a teacher, one who has traveled ahead, otherwise, as the Sufi masters say, your whims will be your teacher. The teacher can help to reflect us and become more aware. For years and years I have not moved an inch unless I thought my four main teachers were present; I did not sit, move eat, drink or speak unless I felt all of them were watching me, and this is the absolute truth. The speed and efficiency with which the microcosm is groomed depends entirely upon our commitment to correct action.

While *tariqa* teaches us inner discipline, our interaction with society at large must be governed by the *din* and *Shari`a* (code of conduct). We are held accountable by Allah for our dealings with other people. Our awareness must extend beyond the self and the immediate environment. *Shari`a* provides clear guidelines for what needs to be done and what should be avoided both on the individual and social levels.

The health of the human microcosm is ultimately dependent upon the wholesomeness of the heart but our interaction with society demands full use of our intellect. Yet there is always argument and conflict in society. Often this causes disappointment. However, this is part of being different; it has to be this way in this world of duality. That is why theologians argue, and why you can almost guarantee that any two mosques or churches will be at variance with each other. However, it is clear that this is not enough; that the intellect with little or no inner light is incomplete.

If we see the unity of attributes, *tawhid al-sifat*, then we understand how the outer reality is an integral aspect of the inner reality, and not separate from it, despite the apparent difference. Otherwise everything conflicts and we cannot cope. Outer laws reflect the inner meaning:

- Whoever applies the outer law without the inner reality has lost the way.

- Whoever is concerned with the inner reality without accepting the outer law is a heretic.

- Whoever unites the two has realization.

We represent *haqiqa* inwardly, with all that entails of light, delight, reality and awareness; and we have to be courteous and bound by the *Shari`a* in our interaction with the world. These are the courtesies of the path. If we commit ourselves to following these prescriptions, then our own actions will transform us. We will be inwardly thrilled and content and outwardly in active service and struggle. We will be human outwardly, subject to making mistakes, and spirit and light inwardly, 'light upon light'.

2: The Self (*Nafs*)

The *Nafs* (Self) in the Qur'an

The *nafs* is by far the most important element in the cosmology of existence. It contains within it the worlds of the heart, the intellect, the drives and the witness. We have seen how it evolves from the original self, the *fitra*, from the fusion of heaven and earth. It is the core of experiential possibilities, but within it is the far greater reality of the *ruh*. The totality of these worlds within the *nafs* are described in the Qur'an in eleven clearly defined batches of *ayat* or verses.

Allah tells us, first of all, that we are all created from one *nafs*, one self. This, as we have seen, means that we all share a basic original design. God then tells us that He created from this one self it's opposite, or pair, which means the duality represented by man and woman. Existence is based on opposites: for every manifested reality, every experience, every feeling, there is its opposite. If this was not so, we would not understand or experience the meaning of anything. We only understand wetness because we also know what dryness means, day because of night, health through illness, good because of bad, and so on.

One set of *ayat* in the Qur'an relates to the *nafs* guiding itself, with Allah's permission, towards right action. These verses show us that guidance comes from within. "And there are signs within your souls" (Qur'an 21:51). God tells us that no *nafs* experiences faith and trust except by God's decree, that is, by His permission and design. There is another *ayah* that states: 'Say that you are not the originator of any good or bad (outcomes) for yourselves' (Qur'an 7:188). In other words, everything comes to us from Allah; we merely filter it through to ourselves, with the option that we accept it or reject it as an experience. In another verse we are shown the inner technology to cope with what we are given in this world: 'If you keep to the correct path of supplication and prayers, giving alms to the needy and spending in the way of Allah, you will find whatever you give of yourselves with Allah' (Qur'an 2:262). Whatever we do with good intention registers with God.

There are also numerous *ayah* that show us how the *nafs* may misguide itself. Allah tells us that within the *nafs* there is an inclination to find attractive whatever state it happens to be in. Indeed, if this tendency was absent in us, we would find it impossible to live with ourselves. If, for example, when angry, this anger seems acceptable to a part of the *nafs*. It is further justified by one saying, 'This is how I am,' even though it is irrational or aggressive. It provides the self with proof of its existence. All of this is geared towards making this self legitimate and giving it a reality. However unacceptable the anger or hysteria, its manifestation means that it must be acceptable to someone. That is why we need a teacher who can tell us which aspect of the self it is. Otherwise we give ourselves excuses. The *nafs* will misguide and deceive us if we allow it to do so. If, however, we spend our time, energy, and wealth in the way of God, we are assured victory over the *nafs* that misleads us.

The Qur'an tells us, however, that our sacrifices and striving are entirely for our own good; that Allah, who is Self-Sufficient, has no need for any of our services. He says: 'And He who sacrifices and works hard is only doing so for his own soul'

(Qur'an 17:7). We are the needy ones who have to purify our lower selves, to shed ignorance and arrogance, to be led by our inner spirit. We need the recipients of our charity more than they need us, in order to learn how to truly serve others, rather than serve our own selfishness. With this guidance that is born out of serving and spending in the manner of the prophets comes light upon the dark *nafs*, like the break of dawn.

The Qur'an contains within it several *ayah* relating to a faculty within the self that keeps a record of all its actions. In this way the *nafs* earns what it does of its own accord and also gives evidence against itself. Ultimately it will live and experience what it has earned. It is as if we are being recorded within ourselves. If we have hidden anything, we are told that in the next realm our limbs and the cells in our bodies will relate our entire life story.

The Qur'an also speaks of the *nafs* containing within it the faculties to check its own mistakes, question its intentions and provide the incentive to change. This applies equally to the individual and the collective. A number of these checks and balances come as trials and what we interpret as afflictions, although they are meant to help us evolve and grow towards our higher potential.

Afflictions, according to the Qur'an, are the result of our own actions that are in turn prompted by the lower *nafs*. Allah says: 'We created man and we know what (evil) his mind and lower self suggest to him. And I am closer to him than his jugular vein' (Qur'an 50:16). The latter part of this statement is an allusion to the unified self, which contains within it elements of the *ruh*, spirit, and the *Rabb*, Lord, who is *Rahman*, all-Merciful.

It is because the original design for all of humanity is one that problems arise when we ignore the spiritual basis of our being and try to impose our personal designs on humanity. But even these trials and afflictions provide us with a means to change ourselves and our habits. Indeed the *Sufi* path, the *tariqa*, is all about change: we are constantly ploughing the fields of our *nafs* and turning over the old soil to make it fertile for spiritual growth. Hence the recommendation that patterns, habits and routines should be broken. One has to change constantly to prevent oneself from getting stale.

Trials also bring with them important lessons in patience for those who recognize God's mercy and generosity in all things. God tells us: 'Certainly We will afflict you with fear and hunger, loss of property and privation. But give the good news to the patient ones' (Qur'an 20:155). When we are afflicted, we must ask Allah to show us where the benefit and goodness lie in our apparently difficult situation. This forms the basis for our personal contract with God. If we know that everything that happens is from the Source of Goodness, then we are given more and more. It also stands to reason, however, that patience is not appropriate when faced with injustice and outright wrongdoing. If it is possible to change a wrong to a right, the situation demands action.

All of this applies to the individual but on the wider social scale any wrongdoing will affect us collectively. We all pay for the disorder of the so-called 'world order', of democracy as a smoke screen for injustice, of individual and national indebtedness. For advanced beings like the prophet Musa (Moses) the price he paid for society's wrongdoing was relatively insignificant. When he and his people were not allowed into Jerusalem for forty years, he stayed in the wilderness. For him it was not so important where he was but rather to serve his Creator and see His Mercy even in deprivation.

Yet change for society as a whole is difficult to undertake in one go. Cultures need repetition to develop traditions which give people an illusory sense of continuity. Change, however, when and if it comes, has to come from among individuals in a society, not for the sake of results, but for ourselves. Our age is a time of spiritual anorexia, when we cannot take the nourishment without rejecting it. However, to denounce our age is to denounce the Merciful God. We have instead to understand our time and the way out of it.

The modern *shaytan* is materialistic and abstract, and so God will give us remedies which will be modern and contemporary to overcome modern sicknesses.

Other categories of *ayah* describing the *nafs* include those that tell us that, within its own limitations, the *nafs* realizes and cares about its own destiny, and will experience what it has earned in its lifetime. Allah also tells us that every self will taste death – separation from its body.

This is a glimpse of the vast vista of the self in the Qur'an. Within this entity called 'you' lie the seeds for the highest spiritual unfolding and awakening given to any creature of Allah. Here also lies the capability to destroy oneself. We need to learn how to protect the original self, by not allowing the lower self to dictate its whims and fancies. This is the reason why maintaining the *Shari`a*, with its protective outer boundaries, is prescribed for us. We may then safely proceed to develop our inner, original, pattern of the self. It will then also become apparent how we are guided from within at every stage as to what is wrong or right. This is not because we want power or psychic abilities, but because this immensity of the self is our true nature.

The Forms the *Nafs* Takes

If the *nafs* is fulfilling its obligation, which is to evolve towards knowledge of its One Source, then it reflects God's plan for all of us; it reflects our *fitra*. If, however, it has been distorted as a reflector, then it takes on the myriad forms that are classified below.

The Commanding Self – Nafs al-ammara

If the *nafs* is completely wayward and has lost touch with its *fitra*, it is classified as *nafs al-ammara*. This is the totally selfish, most egotistical of the selves, which, as the Qur'an says, 'commands to evil' (Qur'an 12:53). It is the *nafs* of the supremely self-centered three-year old child or the despot who wants something and wants it instantly. This *nafs* will not listen to reason or rationality. It is purely whimsical.

The Blaming Self – Nafs al-lawwama

Slightly higher on the scale is the *nafs* whose conscience is pricked because of its bad behavior. As a result, it blames itself for being extreme and may be spurred into positive action in order to do something about its dismal condition. This is the *nafs al-lawwama*, the blaming self.

The Inspired Self – Nafs al-mulhama

If the *nafs al-lawwama* progresses farther along the path,

improving itself, becoming more tolerant and inspired, perhaps even creative, it becomes what is known as *nafs al-mulhama*, the inspired self. It develops a 'live and let live' attitude. It says, 'why not?' or 'It's crazy – let's do it!' Everything goes, even the wildest ideas.

The Certain Self – Nafs al-mutma'inna

When the *nafs al-lawwama* is brought under control, it is on the road to contentment, to becoming *nafs al-mutma'inna*. This self is certain that it will come to faithfully reflect the *fitra* in time, with diligence, commitment, honesty, companionship and applying the right prescriptions. It will increase in its certainty that it has come from beyond time; that it is only here to learn, to experience and to be poised for that final, incredible journey out of the prison of its body.

Allah addresses the *nafs al-mutma'inna* in the Qur'an: 'Oh contented soul, return to your Lord, pleased and pleasing. Enter upon your state of being in adoration of Me; enter My Garden' (Qur'an 89:29). In other words, God is telling this *nafs* to enter into a zone of contentment that is within itself. The root of contentment lies inside each of us so that we may recognize it within creation and become instruments of contentment for others.

The *nafs* encompasses this entire spectrum of all these stages; it can be any of these classifications of the *nafs* or the original *nafs* or self, the natural design given to each of us by God. When we speak in general terms of the *nafs* we mean a state in which we find ourselves at that time.

The prevalent belief that we must renounce the *nafs* is only partially correct. It is only the lower elements in the *nafs* that are to be renounced. This is because the *nafs* is to the *ruh* as the *Rabb* is to God. While Allah is the Source, the Essence, completely beyond anything our intellects can conceive, the *Rabb* defines His lordship over creation. Therefore we can experience *Rabb*, but God in His Essence cannot be experienced in the same way because He is the Giver of experience. In a similar way, God is to *Rabb* what *ruh* is to *nafs*: the *ruh*, like the Essence, is not something that we can understand. Rather, like the visible portion of light that we see along the spectrum of light, the *ruh* reveals itself to us only partially through the *nafs*. If the *nafs* is in turmoil to the extent that the *ruh* cannot accept, then people often resort to suicide, thinking that breaking out of the shell of the body is the only way they can find harmony – *tawhid*.

Grooming the *Nafs*

For the original self to evolve into a reality which is personal to each one of us, the *nafs* must be educated. The most effective way to attain the higher degrees of understanding is by learning the ability to harness the two natural drives of attraction and repulsion.

Every self has within it these driving forces: to us everything is either attractive or repulsive. All of our motivations are governed by either the desire for or repulsion towards a situation, value or object. Whatever we do, whether with the body, mind or higher faculties, is subject to this push/pull mechanism. It is inherent in our nature. The word *nafs* is related to *nafas*, breathing – inhaling and exhaling. Even on this biological level, every organ in our body either takes in what is of use to it or rejects the waste or excess. Whatever we are thinking of we find either agreeable or disagreeable. If we smell a rose, we want to get closer and closer still. While nature has programmed the body to regulate itself to a certain extent, the *nafs* needs education. This is where standards of conduct come to our aid and regulate the *nafs*, until we become self-regulators, learning what damages us and what elevates us. Eventually we find that, of our own volition, we have fewer options, less choice. This is the 'freedom of no choice' that sincere seekers have. We are only truly free from confusion once we are free of choices, when we know there is only one true avenue open to us.

The impetus that moves these two forces is known as the 'driver' (*al-sa'iq*). The driver provides the *nafs* with the energy to make manifest the respective compulsions of these two forces; that is, it gives them reality. Allah says in the Qur'an: 'Every self will come to Us (on the Day of Reckoning) with its driver and its witness' (Qur'an 16:89). Our undertaking as seekers on the path to light is to understand and transform the inner motive, the starting point, of these powers.

The way to do this is to enhance the faculty of 'witnessing' within us referred to in the *ayat* above. We need alertness to witness all our actions and thoughts as they arise within us. It is of little use to see how it all went wrong in retrospect, when it is already too late to do anything about our mistakes.

The Sufi masters, Ibn Sina and Miskawayh amongst others, have codified these powers of attraction and repulsion in great depth. What follows is a complete guide to morals and ethics that can be taken and applied for oneself.

Virtue

Virtue may be defined as that mode of behavior that falls between two extremes. For example, the virtue of generosity is at the midpoint between the two vices of meanness on the one extreme, and indiscriminate giving, or wastefulness, on the other. Nowadays the term 'virtue' has negative connotations, but by being diligent on the path of virtue, by being loyal to the divine blueprint, we end up with hearts that are wholesome.

The Power of Repulsion or Anger

The power of repulsion is also known as the 'power of anger'. When this power is in equilibrium in relation to its opposite qualities of 'fight' on the one extreme and 'flight' on the other, the virtue of courage emerges.

The Power of Attraction or Desire

The power of attraction is also known as the 'power of desire'. Between the two extreme vices of selfishness on the one hand and total abstinence on the other, is the high virtue of modesty.

Interacting and dealing with these extremes is important for gaining knowledge of the virtues, which can then be exercised and experienced. As the individual matures and develops, a stabilizing effect takes place. As this rational self grows, its awareness of the drives becomes more acute as does its ability to rein in these extremes to their respective points of equilibrium. This is recognized as wisdom.

Wisdom comes about as a result of the delicate balancing act performed by all the virtues. The rational self is founded on such wisdom, and combines all the virtues within it. It conducts itself so that it neither harms others nor is harmed itself.

The self and the virtues correspond to make many permutations. Miskawayh categorizes these permutations in some detail, a summary of which is given below.

The Bestial Self

The bestial self is motivated by the power of attraction and its highest potential virtues are modesty and moderation. Modesty in its turn is associated with chastity, tranquility, patience, liberality, integrity, sobriety, the zeal to accomplish good, self-discipline, good disposition, mildness, steadiness, and piety.

If, however, the bestial self remains unpurified, it will sink to its lowest vice of indulgence – the opposite of moderation and modesty.

The Predatory Self

The predatory self is motivated by the power of repulsion and the highest virtue it may attain is courage. From the virtue of courage comes greatness of spirit, which prepares one for major events in life while minimizing their importance in one's own eyes; confidence in the face of danger; the ability to calmly endure happiness, sorrow and even the moment of death; fortitude; forbearance; self-control; what is translated as 'manliness', or aspiring to perform good deeds with the intention to generate good for others; and endurance, using the body for the greater good by adopting good habits and discipline.

The virtue of courage lies between the two vices of recklessness and cowardice.

The Rational Self

The rational self evolves when it follows the path of divine guidance, avoiding the pitfalls of the life of the lower self.

As a result of this self's obedience and submission to the divine reality, it attains the ultimate virtue of wisdom and knowledge. Wisdom gives the self access to knowledge of the divine and the human. It also provides the self with discrimination between what is wrong and right.

Wisdom generates other virtues, the first of which is intelligence, lying at the midpoint between cunning and dullness of mind. Then the powers of retention use what is necessary from the memory and from the imagination, whilst rejecting all that is trivial and of no importance. Rationality develops our ability to investigate the world around us without resorting to frivolity – according too much importance to the study of an object or discipline, for instance – on the one extreme and imbecility on the other. Clarity of understanding, which enhances the powers of deduction, is the median between receiving quick flashes of ideas and an intellect that is slow to grasp concepts. The ability to understand the results of what happened in the past enhances the power to comprehend the 'now', and is the center-point between excessive contemplation that leads to mere fantasy, and deficient contemplation that is of little value. Also emerging from wisdom is the capacity to learn theoretical matters. This virtue lies at the center between a mind that finds learning so easy that it retains little and one that finds learning anything difficult or impossible.

The Combined Virtues

When the three high virtues of wisdom, courage and modesty combine in the self the result is the highest virtue of all, justice.

Justice makes the self fair to itself and others. The just man is im-partial, giving to others what is equally useful for himself. Justice is at the mid-point between the extremes of being unfair to others and suffering wrong at the hands of others.

The virtues that arise from justice are friendship, harmony, fellow-ship, honest dealing, fair play, amicability and devotion.

Justice can only come from self knowledge, otherwise it is superficial. That is why today we have all kinds of competing justices; justice of the strong, justice of the weak, justice of people with money and justice for those without. Then everyone ends up disagreeing and defining terms and we get nowhere. Moral values become eroded and uncertain. Yet Allah created all of man's vices as well as virtues in order for him to evolve along the path to the higher virtues, which in turn enables him to focus attention on the *ruhaniyya*, his spiritual aspect. With this development and unfolding, the truly rational self recognizes ways in which it may avoid danger and harm and achieve stability, well-being and happiness in this world. If we are rotten, selfish, arrogant or vain, then by God Alone we come to know ourselves. Then we begin to know enough is enough; we realize that we cannot satisfy our need for total physical beauty or absolute power. Then we become aware of the One Source, the reason for our creation. It is not an intellectual exercise but it has to be realized, tested and acted on.

'Aql (Faculty of Reason) and Qalb (The Heart)

Within man there is an important faculty called the 'aql, or intellect, which is implied in the above classification of The Rational Self. Its main function is to contain the nafs, by virtue of its reasoning power and rationality. It can only truly do this, however, with the qalb, the heart. The qalb is the higher foundation of the 'aql, and subtler. It takes meaning to a divine dimension, based on love and submission.

Rationality may be learned by acquiring skills of logic and reasoning – the supposed aim of modern education. But a developed person is one who has learnt the purpose of his or her existence; where life is ultimately taking him; what will happen to him after he has passed on from this realm into the next; and how to be fully prepared for this transition. He is also adept at dealing with the world in which he lives, having acquired skills by which he may earn his keep. If we look at the products of today's education, its 'rational beings', we often see men and women whose priorities have been distorted to manipulate and exploit others in order to bolster their illusory existence.

The 'aql remains limited because it operates within the field of causality and rationality which is itself limited. When the 'aql is developed to its limits it will almost extend into the unseen but cannot do so without a qalb that is vibrant and free to guide it from there on. If, in its turn, the qalb is sick or 'rusted' then the 'aql loses its most important abilities: to visualize, imagine, and change values assumed important and erase useless past records and memories. These are three of the five inner senses that are described below.

The Inner Senses of the 'Aql

Just as there are five outer senses, there are also five inner ones.

The first of these is termed common sense, known as *al-hiss al-mushtarak* in Arabic. It combines the senses so that we relate together our abilities to hear and touch, and so on, to gain a complete sensory picture of the outer world in our minds.

The second inner sense is the faculty of *khayal*, often translated as 'imagination'. *khayal* enables us to imagine different forms and formats of things and to place them in different contexts. We can, for instance, through our ability to use *khayal*, 'travel' in our minds from the present to the future. This is a very useful ability in that it encourages us to better our situation or state, using visualization, for example.

Khayal is derived from the Arabic root word, *khayl*, which means 'horse', and it is so named because of the effect generated by a herd of horses as they gallop. To onlookers it seems as if the horses undulate and shimmer as their shiny coats catch the light of the sun, similar to the way in which images flicker through our minds.

The faculty of *khayal* may take a number of forms. We can think up silly images of an animal, for example, whose head is that of a cat, with the wings of a giant bird and the limbs of a human being. By *khayal* we can visualize events from our past in the present.

The third inner sense is called the *wahima*, which enables us to give value to forms or attributes. It is like changing our attitude to someone when we see they have a full wallet, or attributing huge meaning to the printed pieces of paper in it. The *wahima* has to be flexible, as situations change; a one time friend may become an enemy, and vice versa.

The fourth faculty is *hafidha*, the faculty of memory. It is the storehouse of images and experiences from our past to which we have immediate access. We all have memories which are related to the outer senses and to our emotions. This store of memories needs to be constantly purged. Once more, the *qalb* plays a key role in helping us to empty our memory-banks. If we are on the spiritual path and want to protect our hearts, we must forget memories that are irrelevant to us on our journey to enlightenment. We need to 'read' only that part which is of relevance to our lives. Indeed, we instinctively turn away from unpleasant memories and try to remember only what is 'good' from the past.

If we are on the path to the Real, this process of cleansing and purging will take place regularly. Every time we declare *Allahu Akbar* and raise our empty hands in the salat, prayer, we are freed from the past. Just as the body needs to be cleansed and groomed, so does the intellect.

The last inner sense is called *mufakkira* in Arabic. This is the faculty of cognition, or thinking. This faculty can take us from where we are to the unseen zones, with the `aql and the *qalb* working together.

Fikr is a related word, which we defined earlier as 'reflection, meditation, contemplation'. God is continually exhorting and commanding us to reflect. In the Qur'an, there are scores of *ayat* addressing those who are the *mutafakkirun*, that is, the people of reflection. 'And it is He who spread the earth and made it firm with mountains and let in it water flow, and had put in it all fruits. He has made everything in this existence two, and He makes the day to cover the night. Most surely, in all of this there are signs for people who reflect' (Qur'an 3:13). It is in our *fitra* to be in reflection, the most natural state for man. Often, however, we are not reflecting but simply scanning through our past, regretting events that we should have been able to prevent from happening by being more aware of them at the time. If the past can teach us anything, we should take the good from it, ask God for forgiveness and move on. Otherwise the past only serves to clutter our minds.

The main purpose of the inner faculties is to help us relate to our constantly changing world. If our common sense is in a healthy state, our faculty for imagination is reliable, our ability to place values on forms is sound and flexible and our reservoir of information and memories from the past are constantly updated, we may then reflect in an efficient way. Then, too, our affairs will be spontaneously put in order. We will listen for an inspirational signal from our hearts to know what the appropriate course of action is.

3: THE WAYS OF THE HEART

The *qalb*, heart, occupies a pivotal position in the cosmology of the self. It connects man in the seen with the unseen, augmenting the *'aql*, intellect. In it are the capacities to reflect with deep understanding, to retain real knowledge, and to gain far greater insight than our intellects are capable of giving us. The *qalb* is what is nourished by *dhikr*, or remembrance of God. Its health depends on its purity and freedom as far as attachments and worldly matters are concerned.

In the Qur'an when adjectives such as 'healthy', 'wholesome' 'contented' and so on describe the condition of the *qalb*, it implies that these hearts are in dynamic motion and have the ability to reflect the truth.

A large number of other *ayat* describe the 'sick' heart or one that is 'diseased'. The sick hearts are those that find whatever they do attractive. These hearts dislike that which turns them away from the course they are on. They are immersed in fantasy. They are contemptuous. They follow routines and old patterns, doing 'what their forefathers practiced'. The sick heart is also closed, proud, and lacks real understanding for it is engulfed in desire and perversity, constantly in discord and acrimony; hardened and diseased.

The Qur'an tells us that those who look for controversy in their hearts will find it, and will find more and more discord. Also wasteful hearts, those that love superficiality, will want more. Any sickness will be increased.

The Qur'an goes on to describe those hearts that are deadened or sealed. The dead heart is that which is veiled from higher inspiration; wallows in its own turmoil, is cynical and trivializes everything. If such a heart is not treated it will only bury itself deeper, accumulating a rust-like seal over itself.

The hearts of the *munafiqun*, hypocrites, are thus sealed. There is little or nothing we can do to heal such hearts, because of the nature of *nifaq*, hypocrisy. The word *nafaq* means a hole that has several entrances and exits. That is the way of the hypocrite: he enters from one hole and escapes from another; he has many disguises to hide behind. The hypocrite says something meaning something else, causing disruption, confusion, and disunity, when life is about certainty, knowledge, and discovering *tawhid*, unity.

The responsibility to unlock the heart lies with the person who is affected with it. He or she has earned it, either inadvertently or willfully. No one wants a heart that is full of pain, doubt or suspicion. Everyone wants a heart that when it faces its enemy; it is as if, in one's heart, that person was one's best friend. Within the Qur'an, however, there are remedies, all of which point to healing and awareness.

The Inner Heart – *Fu'ad* and *Lubb*

The *fu'ad*, or 'inner heart', is often synonymous with *qalb*. But while *qalb* evokes an image of turning, *fu'ad* pulsates with lucidity, and elevates the intellect towards pure inspiration. 'The *fu'ad* does not lie' (Qur'an 53:32). The word is derived from the root verb, *fa'ada*, to hurt someone in the heart, and *tafa'ada*, to be excited with ardor, to be in motion (Qur'an 28:10).

The Qur'an indicates that the purpose of revealed knowledge is to strengthen our inner hearts (*fu'ad*) and to show us how it experiences life and gives meaning and direction to it. By it we are able to discern the differences between the inner and the outer, between that which is pristine and unassailable, and that which is subject to impurities and confusion. Without the *fu'ad* we would be unable to tell if our *qalb* is dead or angry or tarnished. The *fu'ad* never lies; it is our most valuable state or asset. The *fu'ad* confirms that our main purpose here on earth is to worship our Creator and to know Him. The *fu'ad* helps us to know God; through sight and insight; the outer and inner.

The nature of the *fu'ad* is such that it is always empty and clear like a crystal. The Qur'an narrates the story of the Prophet Musa's (Moses') mother, who had no recourse but to put her baby into a basket and set it afloat on the River Nile to save him from the Pharaoh. In doing so she acted contrary to her powerful instincts as a mother. God tells us that she was able to do so only because her *fu'ad* was 'empty' (Qur'an 28:10). Thus the light of Allah gave her the clarity and courage to act.

With a healthy *qalb* and therefore an empty *fu'ad*, we are told by God that we may have a taste of real gratitude to God. '...God has given you faculties of hearing, seeing and the *fu'ad*, so that you may be thankful' (Qur'an 16:76). If we are in true gratitude, then we do not have any desires or needs. We are at the very source of tranquility, which makes our physical and spiritual faculties poised and at their most efficient, thereby granting us growth in everything we undertake. But the Qur'an also says that very few of us achieve that state of *shukr*, gratitude, implying that most hearts are not healthy.

Although the Qur'an makes no direct reference to *lubb*, or

the innermost kernel of the heart, it speaks frequently of 'the people who have maintained their core'. *Lubb* may be defined as the 'innermost', 'kernel', 'core' and 'essence'. When applied to man, it becomes his very life-substance, the choicest part of him. The word is derived from the Arabic root verb, *labba*, which means 'to remain', 'abide', 'ripen into a kernel', 'to become or be possessed of inner understanding'. *Lubb* is pure and not subject to cupidity or lust.

The word *birr* is closely related to *lubb* in Qur'anic terms. *Birr*, or loyalty, means to 'accept the original blueprint'. It helps us undertake the process whereby we may be loyal to our original *fitra* and establish contact with our *lubb*, the inner kernel, which in turn may give us access to *fu'ad*, the innermost recesses of our heart. *Birr*, then, is the core of our conscience. It will help us discover who we really are and to unveil the root of our origin.

To sum up: if we ensure that our hearts are freed of their attachments and follow the process of *birr* (i.e., accept the original blueprint) by remembering our original *fitra*, we will eventually arrive at the core of our humanity and at the inner essence of our spirituality, *fu'ad*.

We may look at it in another way: While the *lubb* gives us a deeper understanding of our human situation, our *insaniyya*, and the *fu'ad* will lead us to an awareness of Lordship, *rububiyya*.

The Heart, Man and His Spirit

If the heart fulfils its role of reflecting the truth through pure awareness its state is that of pure witnessing, *shahada*. It is a light revealing relevant knowledge. That is why the Prophet, peace and blessings be upon him, said "I have eyes in the back of my head." The *shahid* within us is an accurate witness; it sees our intentions and our actions and captures them all for us instantly, like a snapshot. For example, when we are faced with a dilemma of whether or not to undertake a certain action, we exercise our intellect and reasoning to its limitation and then we need to let the inner heart reflect or indicate what course of action needs to be taken. We must, however, be able to discriminate between the *shahid* and our fears, doubts desires and so on. If we achieve this, we will be rewarded with constant *shahada*. Then, quite naturally, we nurture and revitalize our inner faculties, as these will enable us to interact properly in this world whilst the heart is open to the unseen.

There are three types of *ayat* that refer to the *shahid* in the Qur'an. Some invoke God as the ultimate Witnesser, *al-Shahid*, acknowledging Him as the source of all witnessing. Others tell us that the Prophet also witnesses 'along with those who follow the prophetic path'. The majority of *ayat*, however, refer to the entire creation in the act of witnessing. We are told that our limbs will bear witness, that is, record all that has happened to them in this life, as will our skins. Every cell will testify in a similar way. Everything we do or say leaves its trace in us and around us.

The Monitoring Self – *Raqib*

The *raqib*, or monitory supervising self, emerges when our *shahid* is recording our actions and intentions. This self interferes in our actions to prevent us from causing ourselves harm and duly regulates us. *Al-Raqib* is a Divine Name identifying God as the source of all monitoring and regulating.

The definitions of *raqib* are 'watcher', 'guardian', 'observer'. Nothing is hidden from the *raqib*. The word is derived from *raqaba*, which means 'to observe', 'to respect', 'to watch and wait', 'to watch attentively', 'to fear God'. The act highly recommended by the great masters, *muraqaba*, cultivates self-watching and awareness, which in turn guards us against wrong actions prompted by the lower *nafs*. This is a high degree of meditation that is possible for us to achieve, provided we can enter into a state of no thoughts or feeling, that is, pure awareness. At this stage, we can just be and the *raqib* within us is akin to pure consciousness.

The Recording Companion – *Qarin*

The Arabic term, *qarin*, means in this context 'the recording companion'. Its usual definition is: 'intimate companion', 'associate'. It is derived from the root verb, *qarana*, which means 'to become someone's companion'. *Qarn* also means 'generation', in the sense of 'equal in age', and 'comparable'.

What the word means in respect of the map of the self is defined best in the Qur'an. 'In the afterlife the companion says, "This is what I have with me as a record"' (Qur'an 23:50). The *qarin* reveals its record of our past actions once experienced. The companion is the reality of ourselves at each moment. The Qur'an also warns us against acquiring the *shaytan* as our *qarin*. 'Shaytan' literally means 'to be cast away from the Mercy of Allah'. For people who have made this their *qarin*, this becomes their sole reference point and will mislead them.

We can now clearly see how important it is to nurture the higher elements within the *nafs*, and especially the heart, so that we can deal with our lives on earth in the most efficient way. The faculties of thinking, remembering, imagining, visualizing and the ability we have to transport ourselves from the present to the future in order to transform ourselves in an effective way, all exist to help us achieve this. They also help us to attain our divine potential. A self with a healthy body containing a clear mind and heart can develop and evolve towards the higher.

Insight *(Basira),* Gnosis *(Ma'rifa)* and Unveiling *(Kashf)*

Insight, or *basira,* is the inevitable outcome of a pure heart, clear intellect and healthy mind, with the faculties of witnessing, monitoring and recording in action. This has been programmed into our *fitra* by Allah. God has made creation for us and us to worship Him. We must, therefore, take from creation what we need as provision and turn to the Creator with heart and limbs. But we must passionately want enlightenment and awakening in order to know our *Rabb* (the Sustainer who nurtures us) until passion infuses all aspects of our lives. Passion often gets diffused into relationships but these are only tasters to take us to divine love. God tells us in the Qur'an not to forget our share of this world. But at the same time we need to remember that we are not of this world. This is not being 'mystical', or developing a holy persona; it is transcending pleasure so one begins to unlock the door of indescribable inner joy, using pleasure as a stepping stone to the higher rather than taking bodily pleasures to the point where they destroy us.

The definition of *basira* is 'keen insight' – as opposed to outward vision – 'discernment', 'understanding' and 'the power of mental perception'. The word is derived from the root verb *basara*, which means 'to look', 'to see', 'to realize and comprehend'. God is *al-Basir*, the all-Seer. 'No sight may encompass God'. He cannot be seen yet He is the source of all seeing. It is His will that provides both ordinary sight and insight. The Qur'an says of this attribute of the *Rabb*: 'And He is with you wherever you are.' We want to have access to this attribute of God. *'Ayn al-basira* is 'the eye of insight'. Some Gnostics (*'Ar'fin*) are able to develop this insight to heightened levels, but for most people this insight is non-existent. Like the heart, the inner eye also has its sickness and rust upon it. The Qur'an refers to 'those who cannot see' that is, those who have outer sight but are inwardly blind. Their wrong actions have sealed their hearts so that they are unable to hear or have insight. They are in a state of heedless distraction, unawareness, in *ghafla* – the opposite of being in a state of *dhikr*, remembrance of Allah.

Allah says 'We are closer to all this but you do not see'. This is because we do not look for the source and only see its manifestations. People who continue in their inner blindness will be resurrected blind. Then they will ask 'Why have I been put with these blind people when I had sight in the previous life?' It is because he or she has squandered the opportunity to develop insight, and thereby awakening to the true light behind the play of light and shadow in this world.

God addresses those who are likely to attain gnosis and enlightenment: 'Take heed, those who have insight.' We are told to contemplate the processes of day and night and look for the meaning behind forms and events. We are also reminded that insight, proofs and indications are from our *Rabb*; there for whoever wishes to heighten them. Whoever succeeds in this does so for himself and is granted insight; and whoever fails is blind to himself.

Gnosis – *Ma`rifa*

From keen insight emerges *ma`rifa*, which we may define as 'gnosis', 'realization', 'the ultimate knowledge upon which all knowledge rests'. The word is derived from the root verb, *`arafa*, which means 'to know', 'to recognize', 'to differentiate' and 'to perceive'. The *`arif*, the Gnostic, is he who never sees anything but that he sees the light of God in it, before it, and after it. The wonderful 'crack' of our humanness coming into being as a *fitra*, gives us a wide perspective on all aspects of existence. We gain true knowledge of who we are and where we are going by bringing to the fore our original, higher self and subduing the lower until its *fana'*, literally, annihilation. It is when the person knows that he does not exist independent of his Lord that he is at the door of the Ever-Living.

After gnosis comes a period of inner disturbance and turmoil called '*bala*'. This arises because we feel we do not belong in this realm nor can we escape to the unseen world (for which we have discovered a new-found affinity, having gained knowledge and experience of it).

Once this period of disturbance and uncertainty about outer service is over, the period of simple on-going, called *baqa'*, begins. At this stage we accept all phenomenal existence with grace, seeing it as Allah's infinite mercy in both ease and difficulty.

The *`arif*, or gnostic, is simply one who is awakened and enlightened and thus alive to the moment. A related word, *ma`ruf*, means 'that which is commonly known' – subconsciously we all know that God is the Creator and we are His bondsmen, but we insist on trying to veil this knowledge with fantasies and images of the self. It is this knowledge which was brought by all the prophets and which was known in all earlier systems of belief. The Prophet Muhammad is known as the seal of prophet-hood because he brought with him the additional injunction from God to act and to struggle, both on the outer and within the inner, to do *jihad*; to 'enjoin good, *amr bil-ma'ruf*, and forbid evil. The ultimate good is *ma'rifa*, knowledge of Allah.

The Qur'an gives us numerous *ayat* about 'those who know': they are people who constantly remind, enjoin and encourage people to do good. It is a description of a community that is on the path of gnosis. These are the prescriptions, direction and orders to humanity from God of how we are to live this life: 'They are the people who turn to Allah, serve only Him, praise only Him; who fast and prostrate themselves and bow down; who enjoin good and forbid that which is evil.' Those who have real *iman* will necessarily enjoin what is *ma'ruf*, the ultimate, commonly known good.

A major state in the journey to enlightenment is *kashf*, unveiling from the unknown. This is a high station of gnosis, self-knowledge and enlightenment – the station of the prophets and close followers. God describes it to the Prophet Muhammad thus: 'You were undertaking your journey as a mere human being, unaware of these higher unveilings. It is I who has removed these veils away from you.' At this stage, the sight and insight are sharpness itself. Our *furqan*, the ability to discriminate, is absolutely precise. At this point, the human faculties, *insaniyya*, that are needed to deal with the existential situation – the heart, in particular – are at their healthiest while the spiritual element, our *ruhaniyya*, is exposed to its Creator at all times. Allah reveals what we need to know at the time we need it. The insight itself is clear-sighted. There is no doubt as to what is seen.

4: The Four Facets of the Bondsman

Man is never fully satisfied while he lives in this world because there is something un-worldly in him. His original self, while contained within a physical, material body, is inspired by the non-physical and the unseen. In order to be healthy he needs to maintain a perfect balance between both these aspects. Most of us in this day and age, however, are in an imbalanced state. While our material aspect is well developed, our spiritual aspect is under-nourished. This is why people endlessly seek outer stimulation.

This state of affairs is not natural. Man has a higher need and purpose. He needs to live a life of inner contentment, not simply to 'make do' in the midst of constant turmoil. Most ancient civilizations and cultures understood the spirit in man and its dominance in human affairs. Now there is no comparable ethical or moral standard in our modern societies; only laws that serve the wealthy elite.

What is needed is to base our knowledge on the Qur'an and the prophetic teachings. The way of the Prophet Muhammad is *rahmatan lil-`alamin*, a mercy for the worlds. It is available to all people at all times and is not exclusive to one race or creed, but may be absorbed into all ways of life. The prophetic teachings filter out aspects of a culture that are not natural, thus enabling that culture to retain its own flavor and identity.

The Bondsman (`Abd) of Allah

The Qur'an and the prophetic teachings give us four facets of the `abd Allah, the bondsman or slave of God [Alone], which we will examine in detail in this chapter. When these four facets combine, they provide a complete module of God's highest creation, man, with his potential ability to contain within himself both the human and the divine.

One facet, which may be termed *rububiyya*, deals with the unseen and with Allah's decree emanating from the pre-existential zone before the rise of the human – Adamic consciousness. This highlights God's lordship over creation – God as *Rabb* or Sustainer-Cherisher of creation. From the *Rabb* emanates the personalized spark that we discussed earlier, called the *ruh*, spirit, which in turn generates the original crack of creation, on a microcosmic level, which we identified as the original self, *fitra*.

Out of Allah's countless Attributes comes one that is the most important for us – His being the *Rabb* or 'lord' for each one of us. This Attribute, like all others, emanates from the unseen Essence, which is One and Unique: 'Say God is One...' (Qur'an 112:1) and, 'Your Creator, your God, is One; there is none other than He; and He is the source of mercy...' (Qur'an 2:163).

The Attribute of *al-Rahman*, the Merciful, encompasses all of creation in its mercy, while the Attribute *al-Rahim* denotes an aspect of the *Rabb* that operates on personal and specific levels and relates to individuals or situations. It also contains within itself an element of healing. When, for example, we are ill, we call upon *al-Rahim* for relief from our sickness. However, it is *al-Rahman*, in His infinite mercy, Who allowed us to be ill in the first place; for our own good even though we may not grasp the full purpose and meaning.

The second facet may be termed *insaniyya*, which deals with our human qualities as given to us by God. This includes the faculties of thinking, imagination and the senses.

The third facet is what may be called *ruhaniyya*, the spiritual aspect within us that needs to be strengthened in order to cultivate, and maintain, our links with the unseen. We need to enhance this aspect within us because no matter how much we pamper our human, existential side, we will never be satisfied. Our *ruh* needs to find expression and it does this by making us recognize that we are indeed the center of the universe and that other human beings have the very same potential. This awareness allows us to reach our full potential, and yet recognize our limitations.

The last and most important facet is ʿubudiyya, being Allah's bondsman. It deals with the question of how we are to worship and serve our Creator and how to conduct ourselves in this world and what prescriptions we need to follow. It allows us to avoid transgressing the limits set down by God in His Mercy to ensure we do not become estranged or abusive, but maintain our humanness. It allows us access to a higher potential that knows no limits.

Rububiyya

God's lordship emanates from God's love. God was and there was no creation. He wanted to be known, out of love, and therefore He created. The highest creature in His creation is the human being, both in its form and in its spirit. We are, therefore, in evolutionary terms, at the pinnacle of His visible creation. We are also at the zenith in Allah's unseen realms. The prophets and the messengers who were sent as ideals of their respective times are in advance of us in this respect. We know historical or biographical information about only a few of the thousands that have been sent by Allah to various people at different times as exemplars. Every age, every people had its messenger.

What completes the long line of prophethood, spanning the centuries since the world was created, is the advent of the Prophet Muhammad some fourteen centuries ago. It was during his time, and not before, that *tarbiya*, education in the outer courtesies of living in society, combined with the enhancement of the inner being, was perfected. *Tarbiya* derives from the *Rabb* and His *rububiyyya*.

If we love and understand the Prophet Muhammad and all the prophets and messengers, we will discover their spark and light within ourselves. As we progress towards the higher and the unseen, we will gain more insight into the Prophet's reality. As, too, we are exposed to *rububiyya*, we will understand the essence of prophet-hood. If we know our *Rabb* we will come to know our Prophet, who embodies the original true blueprint, or *fitra*, in all its perfection. We contain it too, although this spark needs to be kindled into a light within us that shines forth brightly. Once this is established, we will not react to external events in an emotional way – seeking results and harboring expectations. Rather, we will respond to these in a state of *tawhid* and become like efficient instruments working to unfold Allah's decree. We become inwardly inspired while at the same time allowing the winds of divine destiny to blow us wherever they will. This condition of being is what we aspire to. Then, if we are on a sure path, we can only evolve more and more.

The Source of the *fitra* and Master of this tremendous creative enactment is called the *Rabb*, often translated as 'lord' or 'master'. The *Rabb*, which is an attribute of God, relates to all creatures and manifestations. The Names of God such as *al-Rahman, al-Rahim, al-Salaam, al-Sabur* and so on, are aspects of the creative *Rabb* that we may experience within ourselves; for we recognize mercy, harmony, peace, and patience. In order to understand *rububiyya*, which is to do with the *Rabb*, we must try and live `*ubudiyya*, which is to do with how we serve our Creator. Creation, then, manifests itself through the *Rabb*. On a personal, individual level, we experience the *Rabb* with our *ruh* – the source of life within us.

There are hundreds of *ayat* in the Qur'an that describe the different aspects of the *Rabb*. These descriptions generally fall into four distinct categories.

One set of *ayat* describes 'those who are guided', consequently giving us a ready made prescription for how to conduct ourselves. One verse, for example, states: 'Say that all your worship, all your adoration, indeed your life and your death are for the *Rabb*' (Qur'an 6:162). This is the voice of those who are guided. They are tuned to the higher principle, knowing that even noble aspirations can only happen if they are part of the decree, if all the elements are right. The final words of the rightly-guided ones, the Qur'an says, can only be 'Praise belongs to the *Rabb al-`alamin*, the Lord of the universe,' (Qur'an 10:10) because there is nothing else to say. Such people recognize the One behind every experience and therefore prepare themselves for growth towards the higher aspects within themselves. They have complete faith in what God has sent to them from His unlimited sources of knowledge, both of the seen and the unseen worlds, and commit themselves to following the example of the prophets and messengers. People who are guided ask God to overlook their mistakes. They know that the lower *nafs* will inevitably lead them astray. Indeed, Allah says in the Qur'an that if He were to hold everyone accountable for the mistakes they have made, there would be nobody left on the face of the earth.

In other *ayat*, God refers to 'those who are established in self-knowledge'. Here the reference is to those who are always vigilant and prepared for their inner light to guide them. As a result of this commitment and discipline, they are honored by God to witness the truth. God describes the Prophet Muhammad, and all those of us who strive to follow in his footsteps, as 'witnesses.' They honestly reflect the truth of a situation.

Allah has sent the Prophet, and those who follow the Prophet's way, to teach people how to achieve this sublime witnessing. We cannot correctly witness unless we are free from the veils of attachments and expectations. This is true witnessing because it is through the eye of the Real (*al-Haqq*).

The next group of references to do with *rububiyya* in the Qur'an is concerned with 'those who deny'. God advises us to call people to the right way, by God's permission, without force or threats. If those who are being called to submit reject what is said to them, we are not responsible for their situation. Some of those who deny are only seeking *dunya* – the power, success, and wealth of this world. Allah says that they will attain some of their desires with no share in the *akhira*, the next world. We are instructed to avoid the company of such people with the words, 'God is enough for me; I am depending on God's inspiration and on His mercy' (Qur'an 9:59).

The third category of verses relates to calling on the *Rabb*. We call upon God, the Essence, but most often we need to call upon our *Rabb*, because we need His lordship to help us with our existential needs. We need to ask for patience, ask our Lord to let our agitated heart be empty. We need to ask our Lord not to make us victims of those who are unjust, and to remove afflictions from us.

The last and predominating category of *ayat* is where the *Rabb* instructs us towards the right course of action. It is the *Rabb*, our Guide and Source in even the most mundane situations in our lives, who gives us direction. If we obey His instructions and give Him due respect, the *Rabb* will grant us 'two gardens' (Qur'an 55:46); one garden, or state, will be experienced in this world, and the other after we leave this zone of time and space.

The *Rabb* tells us to remember our pre-existential original *fitra* by means of which we will come to know our Lord, our *Rabb*. We are instructed, first of all, to follow the rules laid out for us in this experiential, human zone that we inhabit. This brings us into a state of submission and humility and the original self begins to unfold within us and links us to the heavenly, unseen zone. The Qur'an abounds in verses that counsel us to follow the *Rabb's* guidance. We are also told to apply the right courtesy in our approach to the Lord of the Universe, calling upon Him with humility, as the *Rabb* 'does not accept the call of those who are arrogant' (Qur'an 7:55).

It is only with humility that we may dare creep to the door of our Creator's inner sanctum, the courtyard of pure beingness and bliss. One of the points of entry to the door that leads us to Allah is gratitude. God says: 'If you do not thank creation, you cannot thank Me'. That is why we must always thank creation and the prophets, messengers and guides, for they are the perfect guides to the Real. We are to worship Him alone and abide by His natural laws created for our benefit, witnessing His mercy and lordship over all creation.

Tarbiya began from the moment God brought creation into being. This refers to the gathering of the *arwah* (plural of *ruh*, spirit) before they were given outer forms, on which occasion Allah asked them 'Am I not your *Rabb*, your Lord?' (Qur'an 7:172). The original seed of submission to the Real was planted within us long before our concept of time. The *Rabb* is truly the Lord who rules over every situation at all times.

Loyalty *(Birr)*

True submission to the *Rabb* may be achieved consciously with *birr*. God tells us that He has already shown Himself to us 'within ourselves'. This means that we need to dig deep within ourselves where we will find our affirmation to the question, 'Am I not your Lord?'

Those who are *birr* are described in the Qur'an as 'those who reconfirm their origin'. We begin by being faithful to our biological, parental, communal and national origins to some extent, since to deny them is useless. If, for instance, we deny our parents, we deny our biological origin. Even if one's parents were the worst people, we need to forgive them and move on.

We must kindle our sense of acceptance and faithfulness in this world so that we rekindle our total loyalty to the Creator of all worlds.

God defines *birr* in the Qur'an in the following *ayat*: '*Birr* does not simply mean that you face east or west or do your *salat* in a certain way. *Birr* applies to he who has trust in, and knowledge of, God, His Day of Resurrection, the angelic forces, the books of reckoning and decree, all the prophets, and he who performs right actions' (Qur'an 2:177). If we sincerely follow these guidelines, our *fitra* will spontaneously show us what is wrong and right, as we are essentially of a righteous nature.

God also says of those who display fidelity towards Him: 'Certainly, the record and outcome of the deeds performed by the *abrar* (from *birr*) are amongst the highest in God's estimation' (Qur'an 83:18). Elsewhere in the Qur'an Allah describes those who are *birr* as 'righteous ones drinking from cups that make them drunken with the Divine nectar' (Qur'an 72:5).

A great description of the *Rabb* and *birr* comes to us in a quotation from the Prophet Ibrahim in the Qur'an. When asked 'Who is your Lord?' he replies: 'It is He who created me and it is He who will guide me. When I am hungry, He will give me provisions of food and drink. When I am out of balance or sick, He will heal me. It is He who will give me the experience of death and will also resurrect me. He is the One from whom I have the expectation (undeserved) that He will forgive me on the Day of Reckoning. I know that He is all-Forgiving' (Qur'an 2: 258). It is knowledge of one's *Rabb* and loyalty towards Him such as this that leads to the evolvement of the *fitra* in man.

Ruhaniyya

As we have seen, the *ruh* bore witness to the *Rabb* from before existential time. Allah says in the Qur'an that He made man (in the Adamic pattern) and blew into him from His spirit. He also tells us that once this was done, He commanded the angels to prostrate before Adam, as he represented, potentially, the highest created being in creation – potentially, because whilst he is capable of rising higher than the angels, he is equally capable of sinking lower than the animals.

In another verse concerning the *ruh*, God tells us about Maryam (Mary), mother of the Prophet 'Isa (Jesus), who had so devoutly guarded herself from all impurity and dedicated herself to worshipping her Creator. It is said of her, 'We blew into her from our *ruh*' (Qur'an 66:12), hence it is said of 'Isa that he is the 'spirit of Allah'.

God describes those on the path of awakening as those who, after establishing themselves in faith and trust in Allah, gain more in *ruhaniyya* from Him. God says that He will 'increase their spirit with His spirit' (Qur'an 16:102), as long as their faith is always translated into good action.

We know that God's Essence encompasses all desirable attributes in creation. Similarly, God is to *Rabb* what the *ruh* is to *nafs*. We discussed in Chapter 2 that while the *ruh* spans the entire spectrum of existence – the seen as well as the unseen – the *nafs* is restricted to only that which may be experienced in the creational world. We may speak of the *nafs* as being greedy or unjust in a given existential situation only because the light of the *ruh* highlights these qualities within the *nafs*. Indeed the *nafs* only exists because of the *ruh* which energizes it.

Here lies the importance of *dhikr*, remembrance of God. Without it, the *ruhaniyya* in us may remain deficient and under-developed. It is the path to awareness. In modern usage, *tadhkira* means 'passenger ticket', whereas it always used to mean a remembrance or token of remembrance. By remembrance of God we obtain a ticket to the knowledge of God. *Dhikr* offers human beings the divinely sanctioned prescription of rising to their highest potential. With it as a tool, he or she may arrive at knowledge of his *Rabb* and evolve towards becoming Allah's bondsman while being in a state of awareness. We need to be in continuous adoration, for that is our purpose in existence. Spirituality is dependent on inner light, which is why we need periods of meditation and to sit in circles of *dhikr*, invoking God together. In such situations, there is the possibility of experiencing that other quality of life because our bodies are not making their usual demands and our animal self is subdued. If this form of meditation is done collectively, its effect is naturally magnified both quantitatively and qualitatively. Collective *dhikr* circles are a relatively contemporary remedy for the sicknesses of the self and an important part of the spiritual healing process. With regularity and the right courtesy, *dhikr* will help us to transcend the lower *nafs* and bring forth the higher qualities in us.

Ruhanniya is life, light, and gnosis. Life and light are subtly connected. The visible light that we see, and the biological life that we experience, are manifestations of a subtler 'divine light'. God tells us in the Qur'an that there are two lives in this life. The Arabic word for 'life' is *hayat*, which also means 'life-blood', 'vitality'. A related word, *hayya*, means 'to live' or 'experience'. The Divine Name that encompasses all these meanings, and more, is *al-Hayy*, the Ever-Living.

As we have seen, *hayat*, life, is biological and we experience it as such. The Qur'an, however, refers to another kind of life, which enriches and enhances the subtle and spiritual aspect, *ruhanniya*, within us as a counterbalance to the gross and physical.

Indeed, the spiritual element in man is only manifest by means of this parallel life. It is closely associated in the Qur'an with light, giving us a means by which we may distinguish between physical light and a corresponding inner light, or insight. The Qur'an is specific about this enlightened life. Once we awaken to one glimpse of this quality of life and light, we are hooked! We want to remain in that state permanently rather than experience it as a transient state. We want access to it all the time; no occasional glimpses will do. This is how God, in His mercy, entices us and draws us nearer to Himself; to recapture the taste that is imprinted in our sub-genetic pattern, our *fitra*.

Nur means 'light', 'a ray of brightness', 'illumination', 'glow'. It is derived from the same Arabic root word as *nar*, which means 'fire'. A related word, '*munir*', is something that is luminous. The Divine Name that incorporates all of these meanings and more is *al-Nur*, the Light that makes the perceptible visible.

The Qur'an refers to those who are with the Prophet and follow the prophetic teaching shall have their light run ahead of them, and they shall say, "Oh our Lord, make perfect for us our light and grant us protection" (Qur'an 66:8). The reference is to the light of inner guidance which comes through the wholesome heart. We are also reminded of our immense potential and the reward that awaits us if we fulfill this potential: 'It is He who blesses you, and all the angels bless you, so that you may come out of the darkness into the light' (Qur'an 33:43). The best known *ayat* relating to light is *ayat al-Nur*, from the *Sura* of the same name. This profound verse sums up mankind's tremendous spiritual potential.

The on-going life of sweetness that is promised to those who have belief with knowledge, and back it up with positive action, is beautifully encapsulated in this *ayat* from the Qur'an: 'Do not imagine that those who have left their bodies while on the path to God, in *jihad*, are dead; they are living still and being given their sustenance by God...' (Qur'an 2:104). Again, the emphasis is on a life of action, without which we are not allowed to enter the door of enlightenment. Indeed, the Qur'an repeatedly commands us to move forward and act once we understand that we contain a spiritual life and inner light.

Insaniyya

This refers to our physical being. It contains within it the body, intellect and its outer and inner senses and it is dependant on time – on our life cycle. It needs to be enlivened by the *ruhanniya* – the divine element – to reach its fullness. The earliest stages in an individual's life are to do with this physical growth and evolution. Before a child is born, it is completely encompassed in the womb by a unitive state, and yet he or she is not aware of it. We may call this stage in an individual's life as the state of unitive unseen. All existence is unitive; it is to do with *tawhid*. The fetus is in total submission, and is following the program of its development from the unseen to the seen. On the physical level the unborn child is dependent on its mother for food and other biological processes. In this way it is in a state of inner dependence.

With its parents' genetic pattern, a child when born is 'outer dependent' and is aware of its surroundings. Its physical body and co-ordination develop rapidly. As time goes by, the child increases its levels of causal intelligence and learns to become 'interdependent', interacting more with others rather than only with its mother. This process continues throughout its life; it is the stage of maximum mental efficiency, of socializing, and of specialization, but is marked by a desire in its earlier years to seek satisfaction from sources outside of itself.

As he gains maturity and wisdom, man seeks inward satisfaction, realizing that the source of reliable joy can only be found within himself. In fact, at this point the outer world is a reminder and source of disturbance. He becomes more 'inner dependent' again, coming round to a full circle, but this time with knowledge and will.

The First Man – Adam

Now we refer to specific verses from the Qur'an relating to the creation of the first human form, Adam. The name 'Adam' is derived from the word '*adim*' (pronounced adeem), which means 'dust of the earth', referring to our material body and its essential link with the earth. Adam is traditionally regarded as the first awakened being. He is also acknowledged as a prophet in that he had direct access to the unseen while being active in the visible world.

Allah says in the Qur'an that when Adam was created 'he was inspired'. God had planned for him and his wife, his complement, to live in the Garden and take whatever nourishment they pleased from it. The concept of the Garden appeals to us, because the human design is based on the desire for the everlasting garden. We love all that a garden symbolizes; fruits and flowers of different varieties, beauty and the enhancement of such qualities as reflection, quietude, inner peace and joy. It is the meaning and state of the garden for which we yearn.

God goes on to tell us about Adam. The first created man is given a covenant by God that he and generations of human beings after him will come to know their Creator by submission and worship. But Adam forgot this covenant and was 'weak in his resolve' (Qur'an 20:121). This means that in the original blueprint of that creational start, there is an in-built weakness for our own sake, in accordance with God's design. Otherwise nothing would manifest. It is for this reason that we cannot completely renounce the *nafs*. If there was no *nafs*, we would cease to exist. If we did not exist we would be unable to come to know our Source. Our fallibility is part of us, and if we are on a path we become aware of and enjoy our mistakes, rather than constantly knocking our egos. To purify and sublimate the lower *nafs* in order to discover the Higher within us is a noble process. The *nafs*, therefore, is a glorious condition of our existence in this transient zone, just as our bodies are.

Mankind

We defined man, *insan*, as a created being who is tame (*musta'nas*), companionable, and who is able to attain intimacy (*uns*) with God. God tells us that the jinn and the human beings have been created by God only to love and adore and serve Him. Unless we come to know our Creator, we will be unable to fulfill our purpose. No matter how hard we try to arrange the outer world to suit our desire for harmony, it will continue to be in turmoil. Allah does not wish to burden us, but this is our reality. This will be the case until we are able to yield fully to the source of harmony within ourselves. Then the Divine Harmony and Light will engulf and lead us. The weakness that Allah has placed within us is to make us remember our *Rabb* who is Strong (*al-Qawi*). We are created in need so that we may remember the source of all fulfillment.

God tells us in the Qur'an that the most honorable trust, that of knowledge of Allah the Mighty, was offered to the heavens, the earth and the mountains but they refused it, recognizing that they could not take up such a weighty truth (Qur'an 33:72). Mankind, however, boldly took it on, only to forget or cover up this knowledge of *La ilaha illa'llah* – there is no reality except God Alone. *Insan* forgets or covers up this knowledge because he cannot bear the incredible weight of his own non-existence. He sees himself at all times and forgets his source. He looks at the shadow and does not see the effulgent sun. This is why we are mostly in shirk – imagining that anything exists beside Allah. As weakness and forgetfulness are part of the spectrum of *insan*, we can remind ourselves in times of weakness that all of us are at a loss, and that God is all Forgiving. All we need to do is return back to the path of awareness and remembrance and recognition, because this is within us. In fact the Arabic word *istighfar* is wrongly translated as seeking forgiveness. It means to ask for the effects of our faults to be covered over. It is more than forgiveness; it is being rendered whole.

'Ubudiyya

'*Ubudiyya* is based on the development of the rational self through outer action. Ultimately this is the recognition that we are of no significance unless it is because of the divine program that began before our involvement in it. We are already slaves to this reality. The use of the word 'slave' however, implies oppression and exploitation, which is not true of the Arabic word '*abd*, from which comes '*ubudiyya*, servitude or obedience to God. The meanings encompassed by '*abd* include 'that which is smooth' or 'that which creates no friction.' The '*abd* is content because he knows that he truly belongs to the *Rabb* and controlled ultimately by a loving Lord. The relationship is that of mutual complementarity and symbiosis. The root verb is '*abada*, to render easy, implying that that to truly submit to the primal decree is to allow ourselves ease.

By nourishing the *fitra*, making it the guiding principle in our lives, we will become '*abd*, bondsmen, to the Real. We are then in a state of '*ubudiyya*, the state in which the Creator designed us to be. Our *fitra*, which encompasses all our human faculties, and our *insaniyya*, will lead us to interact properly in the world. Our spiritual faculties, *ruhaniyya*, meanwhile, will receive appropriate inspiration from the unseen world. Thus we encompass the seen and the unseen – the worlds of form and non-form.

Allah illustrates the different aspects of '*ubudiyya* in the Qur'an. Through these *ayat*, we are given indications of how '*ubudiyya*, when it is fully evolved, can reflect *rububiyya*. We contain the essence of both within ourselves. Indeed, our *Ruh* is from the Light of God.

God reminds humankind that we are created in such a way that we will continue to strive towards our Lord until we meet Him. In other words, whatever we strive for, we are in reality trying to attain knowledge of our *Rabb* and His ways. In this way, the lowly bondsman reflects the highest reality, which is Lordship, *rububiyya*.

There are three types of *ayat* relating to the bondsman in the Qur'an. The first category speaks of the good `*abd*, for example: 'The bondsmen who are sincere in their attempts (to please their Lord) shall have a regular provision' (Qur'an 65:11). This does not apply only to our means of livelihood. The 'provision' spoken of here is like having access to a tap that we may turn on when we need to be nourished by the waters of the Garden. It gives us the ability to enter the inner Garden within ourselves, with its gifts of joy, tranquility and infinite peace. This is the 'provision' to which God refers. If we reach our inner Garden through awareness, meditation and true submission and achieve total inner silence, then we stand at the very edge of that zone in which lie infinite peace and bliss.

The Qur'an refers to the light of guidance that God provides for the `*abd* who is sincere and who qualifies for it. By emerging out of the darkness of past memories and future anxieties we shall begin to see the light of the present. If we remain in darkness we will get only what is appropriate for that zone: ignorance, bickering, disputes and doubt. The Qur'an speaks of those bondsmen who are on the path of success, those who are grateful, who are constant in their praise of Allah, and who seek out knowledge of the meaning, purpose and origin of existence. Each moment is an opportunity to either rise with knowledge or sink with ignorance. This knowledge is at first informative but its effect will only become experienced when we are transformed by action resulting from this knowledge.

Another type of verse relating to `abd describes 'those who are at a loss'. They are confused, blindly following tradition and old patterns, although these are founded on ignorance and corruption.

The third category of *ayat* comprises what Allah expects from His bondsmen. Here are Allah's warnings to the bondsmen, of His prescribed limits and bounds, His purpose and His decree. At the same time we are told of His gentleness towards His creation. We are reminded that it is God who gives His bounties and gifts to creation as He sees fit and according to our needs, and not according to our whimsical desires.

From *Rabb* to `Abd

There is true proximity between the *Rabb* and the `abd, but never a union as such. It is like coal and fire. When coal is close to the fire, it takes on the qualities of the fire and exhibits these to the onlooker. It is all light and brilliance. If the coal is removed from its proximity to the fire, it becomes just that – a lump of coal. `Ubudiyya faces *rububiyya* like a mirror, enhancing it and making it evident. If the `abd was not manifest in this existence, the *Rabb* would not be manifest, and vice versa. One needs the other; indeed one cannot exist without the other.

Real submission and faith leads to real `ubudiyya by grooming and proper upbringing, *tarbiya*, in the real sense of education. True education means learning a few skills to earn one's keep, and ultimately about knowing the purpose of our existence, and preparing for death and beyond.

The *Rabb* comes into existence from the One Source, the Essence, only as an intermediate step to bring about the orchestration of existence, paving the way for the `abd to be brought up to his or her full potential. `*Ubudiyya*, for its part, makes us recognize that we have within us the original blueprint that enables us to develop into true reflectors of the *Rabb*, whilst also training us to exercise our faculties and senses to gain the greatest benefit from them.

Imam 'Ali says of combining the lower and the higher faculties in this way: 'I see two aspects of `*aql*: one that is designed (by God) and imprinted in you; the other that enables you to hear, see, and interact.' The implication is that without the original blueprint, the sensory faculties are only of superficial use. If the seed of intellect was not already within us, the `*aql* would not have the possibility of developing. Indeed, the reason for using the senses is precisely to enliven and bring our *fitra* to the surface, making our dealings with the world as trouble-free as possible.

Action and Transformation

As we have seen, *Rububiyya* is related to the Essence and corresponds to *haqiqa*. *Insaniyya* and *Ruhaniyya* are related to our earthly existence and the spiritual elements within us, corresponding to our path, our *tariqa*. The development of all these elements requires action that will transform us. If we fail to act appropriately, we will not be inspired enough to recognize our true purpose on earth. If we fail to acknowledge earth, we will not gain access to heaven. The higher rests on the lower, while the lower has emerged from the higher.

This zone of existence is all-important: it is here that we develop our human qualities as well as our divine potential; here, too, where we make our mistakes, are given our prescriptions and remedies, and here that the healing process takes place. Here we are accountable to each other for our actions, and here we help or hinder each other. This is the foundation of the world, of the self, of creation as a whole. It is in this realm of *`ubudiyya* that we make the correct start and follow the shortest path to transformation: Islam, *Iman* and *Ihsan*.

We must not forget also that we all have an appointment with death. But is that the end of our story? Allah tells us it is not. In fact, it is only the beginning. This world is the opportunity we have been given to chisel our future existence as it will be, once we have moved on from this multi-dimensional world limited by space and time. At that stage, we will be a self in the world of the unseen. Because that next world is beyond time and space – in that time and space do not contain it – we call it 'forever' or 'eternal'. Eternity is non-existent time. In our current existence, we have the ability to act and interact. In the *akhira*, the next world, we will be unable to do so.

The Bondsman in the Arena of Action (*`Amal*)

The bondsman naturally needs an arena in which to act, so that the world of creation and the meaning behind it is connected. It is futile to obtain a prescription from the doctor and not apply the remedy suggested. There needs to be a commitment towards healing the ailment and application of the cure. If this is done, then transformation will undoubtedly occur. All that we have discussed so far, regarding the different elements within our inner cosmology, will come to the fore: our *insaniyya*, our *'aql*, our *ruhaniyya*, the seen and the unseen, will find their meeting point within us. We will then understand what the Sufis mean when they say we are 'in this world but not of it'.

Action with reformed direction, then, is the key. It is the proof of our commitment to the prescriptions that God has written out for us in the Qur'an. The *ayat* concerning *'amal*, action, fall into definable categories. There is a great deal of emphasis placed on 'the right action'. We are told that he who acts righteously will receive a reward that is greater than it, while he who acts wrongly will only taste its consequence (and no more.) Elsewhere in the Qur'an we are told that our good actions will 'wipe out' misdeeds. Nature gives us some leeway after we have committed an error: results of wrong actions are often delayed. This is so that we may repent, correct and try to make amends. If we do this, the wrong action will indeed be 'wiped out'.

We have to remember that the highest action is the one that is undertaken for God alone with no expectations, recognizing that it is ultimately by God and takes us towards God. There can be no deed higher than this. God assures us that such action will only bring increase. If, however, we do wrong without keeping this higher intention in mind, we are wronging ourselves. That is God's mercy and balance in this world. Good deeds serve to generate further right action and our state in the next life will be none other than a manifestation of our actions in this life.

Our actions are recorded by our 'recording companion', irrespective of whether we are conscious of this at the time or not. The recording takes place in every cell of our bodies. Perhaps the most beautiful verse concerning action incorporates much of what we have discussed so far. It says: 'Whoever performs good deeds, and he or she is a believer, We most surely will make him or her live the happiest of lives, and We will most certainly give as their reward better than what they did' (Qur'an 16:97).

This is the 'good news' that the Qur'an brings to the true *mu'min*, the believer. There are right actions and wrong actions, and we have, ostensibly, the freedom to choose to undertake either. And yet, we are programmed wanting goodness, happiness and enlightenment. It would be the ultimate folly to let this divine opportunity pass us by.

Salat – Prayer

God tells us the best of all actions is *salat*. It is the solution to the problem of shirk, seeing oneself rather than bearing witness to God. The Prophet Muhammad said that shirk is so subtle, it is like trying to catch a black ant on a black stone on a black night. It means that if we do not see the One, then we are not unified within ourselves. Then whatever we do will be of no use. We would have no unitive understanding. There can only be one Lordship, otherwise there would be different messengers with conflicting messages. However, the prayer, *salat*, is an efficient way of diminishing our confusion. The ultimate aim of the *salat* is to make ourselves disappear in prostration (*sajda*): we do not exist any more. During prostration, we acknowledge our non-existence and the fact that God was, God is and God will be

Ever-Existent.

The Path to Knowledge

We have seen how *insaniyya*, our human aspect, is founded upon the physical body, which is moved along over a period of time to the subtler, higher realms of thinking and reflecting. This continues until man reaches a state of `*ilm*, knowledge, as distinct from information.

`*Ilm* is defined as 'knowledge, learning, certainty'. The word is derived from `*alima*, which means 'to know, to be cognizant of, and to be aware'. The Divine Attribute that encompasses `*ilm* is al-`*Alim*, the Omniscient.

`*Ilm* is the certainty we all seek. For instance, if we know for sure that when we are abusive we will be abused in turn, we will refrain from abusing others. The awareness of the consequences will in itself provide the necessary protection for us. To be given this type of awareness, we need to call upon al-`*Alim*, recognizing our limitations with all humility. To begin with, we may gain outer knowledge; to do with our existential situation. As we progress, we will gain higher knowledge, subtler awareness and unveilings.

The verses referring to `*ilm* in the Qur'an can also be grouped into distinct areas. One selection teaches us that God is the root and source of all knowledge and that He alone encompasses all aspects of `*ilm*. Often, this omniscient attribute of Allah is linked in the Qur'an with His Attribute of *al-Sami'*, the all-Hearer who is also the Responder. He has knowledge of us and will hear and respond to our real needs, as we progress towards Him, by Him.

God Alone knows best what is suitable for us at any given

moment – better indeed than we know ourselves. Human knowledge is extremely limited and we are 'given (of it) only as much as we need'. We only need to know enough to see us through a single moment at a time. We do not need mountains of extraneous information cluttering up our minds. Knowledge is based on utilizing appropriate information at each moment to maintain the correct relationship with the All-Knowing.

Knowledge comes to us from God through commands, signs, examples and parables (Qur'an 96:4). Every creational situation has in it Allah's Word because it emanates from the One who commanded *Kun!* – 'Be!', the word that is used by the Creator to bring things into being.

Allah commands us to uphold what is already known; that there is One Essence behind all realities. At the same time we must not mix up truth with falsehood, nor hide the truth that we know.

The Qur'an tells about 'those who know' and 'those who do not know'. Those who know are constantly vigilant about what God wants of them. They are in submission and have no other option except to yield to the decree and therefore experience and welcome destiny. They live in the moment and therefore cannot but be in the right place, doing the right thing at the right time. These are the bondsmen of Allah who can be truly said to possess knowledge, because they are cautiously aware all the time of the creator who permeates all existences and who is the master of Time.

Conclusion

The entire discipline of the path is the *din*, or 'life transaction.' It is the path of God, the way of nature, and we all want it. It is the totality of knowing that inwardly we are beyond time and space, but outwardly we are constantly striving to struggle for the good and condemn what is bad. This is what is meant by the phrase *fi sabil Allah*, in the way of God. It is active, giving the best that one has, being willing to change, and constantly improving, so it becomes a way of life. It is quietening the mind and grooming the self. It is for this reason activities such as gambling are forbidden because they are counter-productive to inner joy and outer courtesy, which leads to greater and greater insights and greater and greater guidance until one reaches the Source of Guidance. This is living in the moment.

True Sufism is this science, but it is not about worshipping Sufism or Islam. We need the Muhammadi path, the way of all the true prophets, but ultimately it is about our access to that constant awareness and remembrance of the one and only Source from which comes the ultimate yardstick and that is Allah. The path is the car driving to the city, and the city is the city of light. We need to give the right signals and we need to check that the mechanical parts of the car are working. That is the humanness. We need the electrics to be working, as well as our inner charge. That is the *ruhanniyya*. But if we get stuck on healing or self knowledge, or comparing teachers, it is like stopping at the service station forever, tinkering with the car, instead of driving.

We are all going to die! We only need self knowledge and healing in order to arrive. We need a teacher to point out the falsehoods that we ourselves have built, but only God can give us truth, truth that is already within us. The truth is that one knows God by God, and one knows people of God by God. The closer one is to Truth, *Haqq*, the more one knows the people of *Haqq*. Imam 'Ali said to the Prophet, 'I know you by God, and I recognize you as the Prophet.' So the higher you move, the more you come to realize this truth. The Prophet Ibrahim knew that Allah would give him what he needed when he needed it. But are we ready? Are we true servants? Are we the coal that is light upon light because of its proximity to Light?

God has created the essence and the means, so we have to ask if we are willing to take it, to be greedy for light, and get to the city. Knowledge of God comes from God and by God, and God is *Rabb al-'Alamin*, that which has to do with existence. What we have dealt with here is existence. God is pre-existence, and gives the power and light to existence and post-existence, and that is what we need to discover.

A Glossary of Key Terms

Below is a unique collection of terms that have been handed down to us over the centuries to make it easy for us to grasp the inner workings of the self. All of these terms are based on the Qur'an and the way of the Prophet. Many of the terms echo those found in sacred texts written in ancient languages, such as Sanskrit and Hebrew. These are known as the 'Adamic languages' and seem to be imprinted within our deep consciousness. If we allow it, if we move through the false barrier of language, then the terms defined below will resonate within themselves and unfold their individual meanings. Then we can leave behind the value-laden terms of the present day and access the full spectrum of the cosmology of the self.

Allah God; the Greatest Name of God; literally 'the god'. He is the Source from which, and to which, all things emanate and return. This one Name incorporates all the Divine Names, the Most Beautiful Names of Allah, such as *al-Awwal*, (the First) *al-Akhir* (the Last), *al-Zahir* (the Manifest), *al-Batin* (the Hidden), and so on.

Allah is the root of the manifestations of Attributes and all that emanates from Him in our visible creation, and in the unseen realms. We cannot define Him. The Prophet tells the believers not to speculate about Allah's Essence, but we can learn His Names and speak of His Attributes and the way they manifest in our life on earth. Indeed we are able to discuss and observe because of Allah. We are His project; not the other way around.

'Aql The faculty of reason, intellect, discernment, rationality, mind is derived from the root verb *'aqala*, 'to restrain a camel by tying its forelegs together; 'to confine, to be reasonable'; 'to understand'. The implication is that true rationality and intelligence can be cultivated only if the lower *nafs* or self is restrained. This is because the *'aql* has an innate quality of being rational and will not permit the lower elements of the *nafs* to run riot within us. It has the ability to restrict and limit us in order that we may gain access to the Limitless. The use of the *'aql*, with its rational approach, provides us with the first stepping stone towards that Reality which is beyond reasoning. It is founded on the five inner senses.

Ard The earth, land, country, soil. The word 'earth' may have been derived from this. *Ard* is distinct from *dunya* (see below). It signifies a neutral surface, providing us with sustenance, interaction, experiences, skills, and mobility for our learning and growth.

Dunya The world as we experience it. Closely related to *ard*, the latter becomes *dunya* when human beings interact with it, and our perceptions and emotions are added to the equation. *Dunya* suggests worldly possessions and attachments. The word is derived from *dana*, 'to be low or near; to be base or vile'. Some of its derivatives include *adna*, meaning 'that which is baser than other things, or more vile, degraded'; *hayat al-dunya*, 'the life of this world'; which is ignoble and base as opposed to that of the *akhira*, the next world.

Din is the natural path which leads to understanding the ways of our Creator through faith and submission where human beings are an integral part of the unitive process, of *tawhid*. It is the transaction between the Debtor (Allah) and the indebted (human beings); the life-transaction itself. The word is derived from the root *dana*, which means 'to owe, to be indebted, to take a loan from, to be in an inferior position'. To live in the *din* implies repaying one's debt to the Creator with the honor and dignity that befits humanity's high station in creation. This key term is often translated as 'religion', which does not transmit the full range of meanings of the original Arabic. Whereas 'religion' is often synonymous with structural tyranny and terror, the *din* is a means of transacting in harmony with the rest of creation. Organized religion, including Islam under the despotic control of some so-called Muslim countries has become a system of legitimizing power and control. But behind the veil of the ever-confusing behavior of some Muslims is the universality of real Islam and the Qur'an.

There is only one *din*, one method of abandoning falsehood and discovering truth. The Prophet Muhammad and numerous other prophets and messengers expounded this truth to different people at different times. *Din* is about inner purification, and correct action on all levels; it encompasses both *shari`a* and *haqiqa* and brings about transformation of the individual and society.

Fikr is reflection, meditation, contemplation. From the root *fakara*, to reflect, cogitate, ponder, and think.

Fitra This is man's natural disposition; his innate nature; the human blueprint and the natural composition of the child created in the mother's womb. *Fitra* is derived from the verb root *fatara*, which means 'to split, to cleave the flesh and come forth, to originate, to create'.

Fitra means a bringing into existence and originating. It indicates an original blueprint according to which such a 'bringing into being' may take place. The Qur'an tells us that if we fail to acknowledge this fundamental feature of our life on this earth, we will suffer here and in the next world. This suffering is the process of purification called *adhab* which is commonly translated as 'affliction' or 'punishment'. This affliction is founded on Allah's all-encompassing mercy. We are afflicted in order to be moved to the right action; engaging our *fitra* by applying the principles of the *din* within ourselves and in our dealings with others.

Iman This is faith, trust, belief, acceptance. The word is derived from *amana*, 'to believe', and *amina*, 'to be tranquil in heart and mind, to become safe and secure, to trust'; also, *amana*, 'to render secure, to grant safety'. Derivatives of the word include *amn*, 'peace, security, protection' (the opposite of *khawf*, fear); *amin* (pronounced *ameen*) 'he who is trustworthy, faithful, honest' – it is one of the names of the Prophet Muhammad, who embodied these qualities; *mu'min*, 'a believer, he who is given certainty and trust'. *Iman* is being true to that with which Allah has entrusted us, firmly believing in all He asks us to believe within our hearts, and not by merely professing it with the tongue.

Our *iman* begins by simply stating it. We believe and have faith that Allah did not create us and our world in vain. We also have faith that creation is not in chaos and without direction or purpose. In order to perfect our *iman*, our hearts must experience how we fit in as a locus between the seen and the unseen; realizing that the ups and downs of physical reality serve as a screen on which the unseen projects itself in many ways. This is the second stage of *iman* in the heart, experiencing the world through our own senses and understanding its higher meaning through our heart.

The *mu'min* becomes aware that everything from Allah is perfect, even though in the worldly turmoil and confusion he or she may not immediately be able to see this perfection. He then asks Allah to show the mercy and meaning in whatever apparent difficulty or trial is taking place. Our *iman* will be like a torch lighting the way for us, until we see by it alone, rather than by speculating with our intellects and through past experiences. There comes a time when the heart is totally effulgent and we ourselves become manifestations of *iman*.

Insan Man, human being, one who is tame as opposed to being wild. The additional characteristic of *insan* is to be a container for the *nafs*. It is this property that dictates physical appearance. The word is derived from the root *anisa*, which means to be compassionate, sociable, friendly. Derivatives of *insan* include: *insaniyyah*, 'humanity or the condition of being human'; *musta'nas*, 'tame'; *uns*, 'intimacy'. One school of philology finds that the word is related to *nasiya*, which means 'to forget'; having been entrusted by Allah to be His vice-regent on earth, man forgets his real purpose and fails to fulfill his duty.

Related phrases comprising the word *insan* include, *insan al-kamil*, 'the perfect or complete man'. This is the cosmic man; one who has recognized the limitations of the self – the microcosm – and has also heard the echo of the macrocosm within himself. The macrocosm is referred to by the Sufi masters as the *insan al-kabir*, literally, 'the greater man'; the whole of creation.

Islam is submission to the Will of Allah. The word derives from *aslama*, 'to commit oneself'; *salama*, which means 'to be safe and sound, unimpaired, intact, blameless, to be free'; *sallama*, 'to preserve, deliver, salute'. The Muslim is he who trusts Allah and submits to Him. Islam must be established before faith, *iman*, can yield its fruit.

Ihsan When one is firmly established in Islam and *iman*, the light of *ihsan* will shine. This is the state in which we do not see Allah but are certain in our knowledge that He sees us. It is as if we are Allah's guests, abiding within the house of the King of kings. We are aware of ourselves and conduct ourselves impeccably. This is even more the case when we find ourselves in the Presence of the all-Seeing, the all-Hearing, all-Knowing Creator. This is called *maqam al-ihsan*, the station of *ihsan*. The triad of *islam*, *iman* and *ihsan* presents us with what action to take to proceed in our quest for knowledge of the Real.

Kufr Denial or rejection of the existence of Allah; absence of belief, ingratitude. The word is derived from *kafara*, which means to cover, to hide, and to be ungrateful'. The *kafir* denies the existence of Reality and covers over the truth. Indeed the word *kufr* gives us the word 'cover' in English. Another related word is *kaffara*, which means 'making up for loss of some kind'; to 'render something neutral'; 'to make reparations or amend for what may have been done inadvertently to cause harm'.

Nafs The self, soul, psyche, mind, the human being. The meanings of *nafs* include man's innate nature, his genetic predisposition and naturally conditioned behavior. The *nafs* may manifest itself as being base and animalistic or spiritually elevated, depending upon its state of purity. The word is derived from *nafis* (pronounced *nafees*) 'to be precious, valuable'; *naffasa*, 'to relieve, to comfort, to air, to uncover'; *tanaffasa*, 'to breathe, to pause for breath and rest'. *Nafas* means 'breath'. *Nifas* means the time shortly after a woman delivers her baby.

Qalb The heart, the middle, core, center, pivot. The word is derived from the verb *qalaba*, which means 'to turn, transform, transmute, tilt'. *Inqilab*, also derived from the same root, means 'revolution'.

According to Sufi traditions, the heart has to constantly revolve and be ready to return to its Creator. While our overall worldly objectives may lead us along a particular course, our heart must remain unattached in order to be in the healthy and wholesome state referred to repeatedly in the Qur'an. There are many *ayat* in the Qur'an that describe the ailments that may affect hearts and make them 'sick', such as doubt, anger, suspicion, and so on. We have to move and turn constantly to prevent the heart from becoming fixated on one thing.

Allah says in a Hadith Qudsi (a sacred tradition), 'I created the earth and the heavens for you, and I created you for Me'. If our heart is free of attachments, we become true creatures of Allah and are able to see Allah's decree with clarity. Then we may fulfill our destiny in the most harmonious and perfect way.

APPENDIX

Notes on the diagrams

The following diagrams are condensed sketches of the various aspects of the dimensions of the self. They are helpful after reading the text. They can only be fully understood if one looks at them in a dynamic and integrated fashion.

Our attempt in presenting these diagrams is to show the multidimensionality of the self. At one end, it is earthy and limited. Yet at the other end (both ends in fact - the beginning & the end), it is from a zone of limmitless, boundless & undefinable aspect of light.

Zone of essence.

This is where it all begins and ends. This essence is undefinable & undescribable. Yet it is the root of all attributes & manifestations. All existential realities are based upon the all-pervading zone of essence that encompasses the world of seen & unseen.

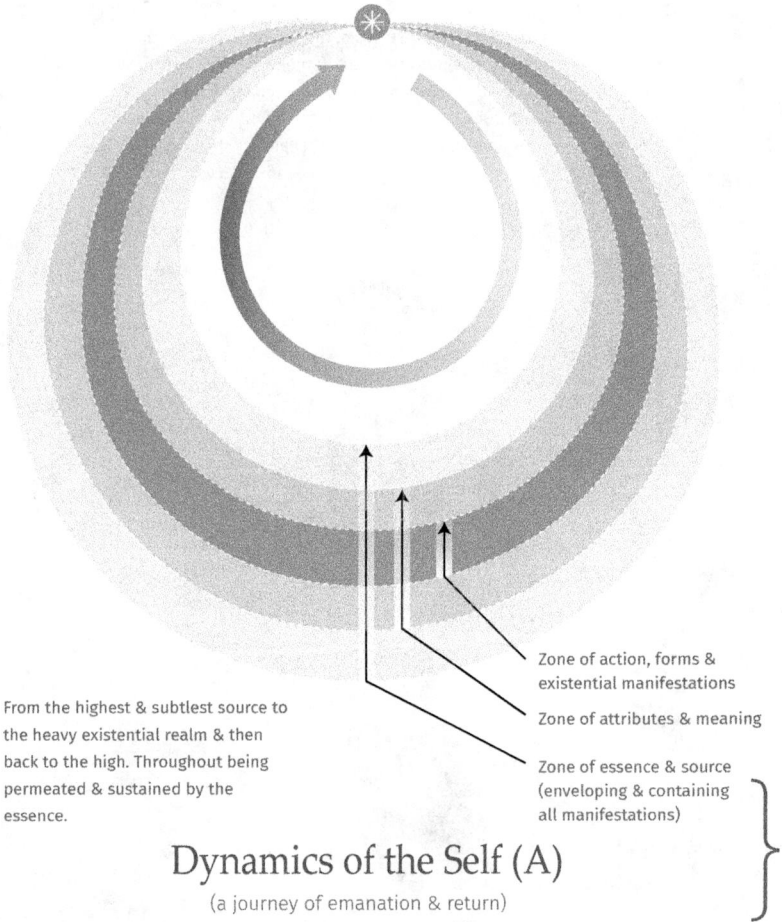

Zone of action, forms & existential manifestations

Zone of attributes & meaning

From the highest & subtlest source to the heavy existential realm & then back to the high. Throughout being permeated & sustained by the essence.

Zone of essence & source (enveloping & containing all manifestations)

Dynamics of the Self (A)

(a journey of emanation & return)

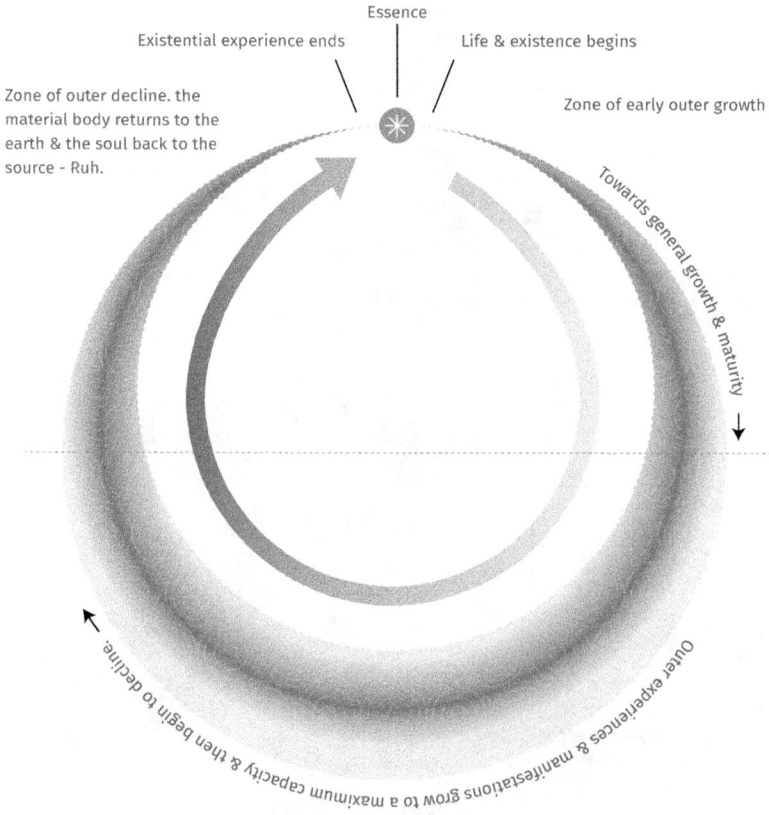

Essence

Existential experience ends

Life & existence begins

Zone of outer decline. the material body returns to the earth & the soul back to the source - Ruh.

Zone of early outer growth

Towards general growth & maturity

Outer experiences & manifestations grow to a maximum capacity & then begin to decline.

Dynamics of the Self (B)
(emanation & return)

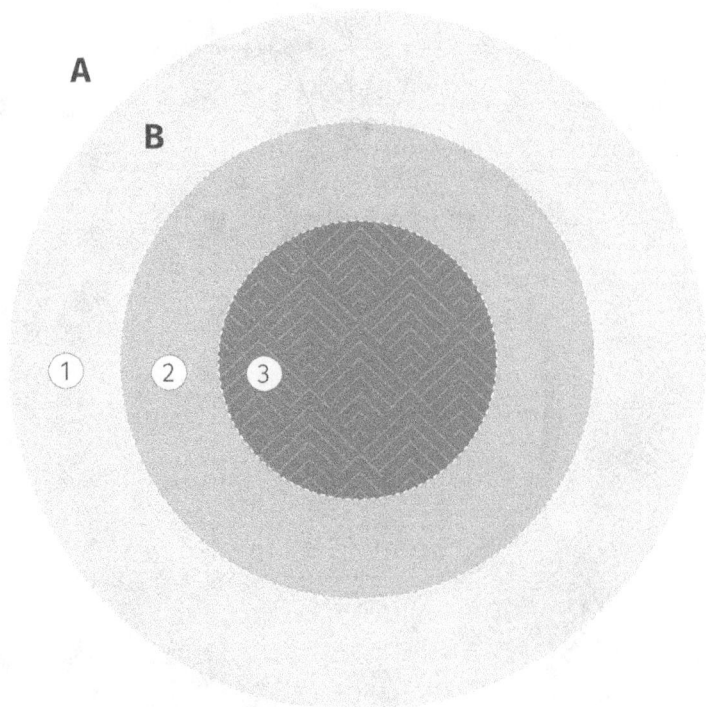

A. Unknown & unseen & pre existence & manifestation

B. Creational reality with its three main zones or dimensions.

1. Zone of essense & source. (Spirit)

This zone contains and controls 2 & 3. (Subtle & all encompassing).

2. Zone of attributes & meaning. (Soul)

This is the zone off attributes & meanings which gives rise to form, structure & existential experiences 3.

3. Zone of action, forms & existential manifestations. (Persona)

This is the world of experiences, the outer senses & all physically and materially describable realities. It is dense & structured in its appearance.

Dynamics of the Self (C)

(a cross section)

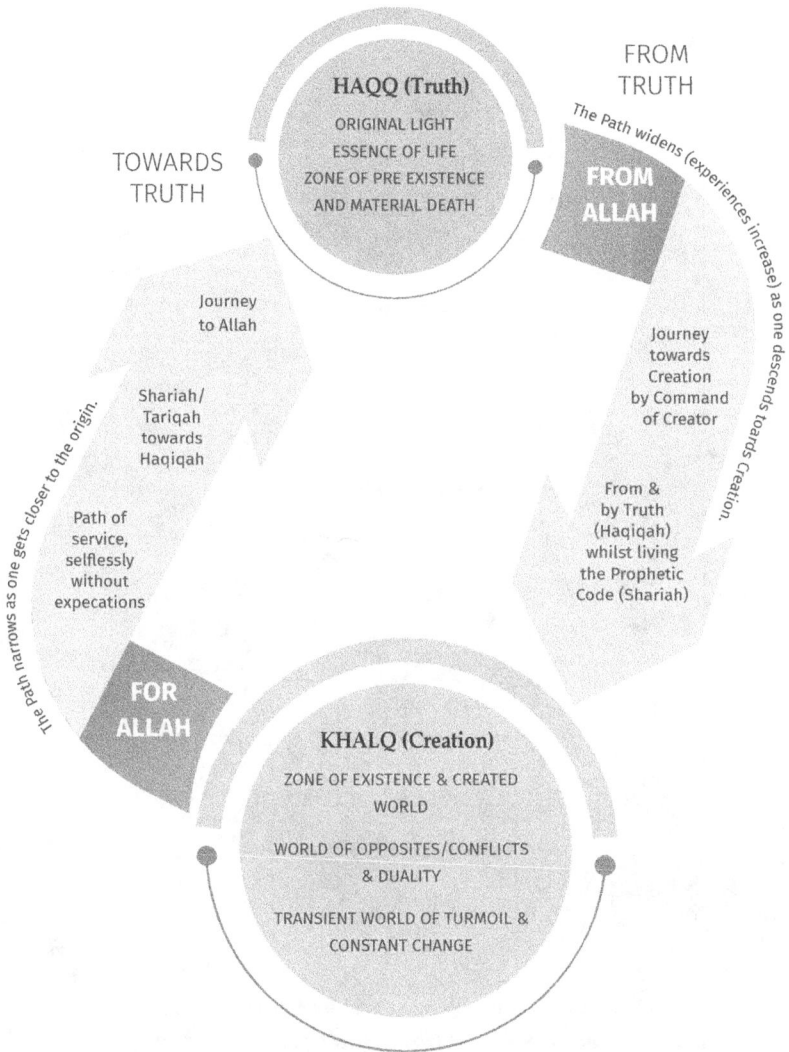

HAQQ (Truth)

ORIGINAL LIGHT
ESSENCE OF LIFE
ZONE OF PRE EXISTENCE
AND MATERIAL DEATH

FROM
TRUTH

TOWARDS
TRUTH

FROM
ALLAH

The Path widens (experiences increase) as one descends towards Creation.

Journey
to Allah

Shariah/
Tariqah
towards
Haqiqah

Path of
service,
selflessly
without
expecations

Journey
towards
Creation
by Command
of Creator

From &
by Truth
(Haqiqah)
whilst living
the Prophetic
Code (Shariah)

The path narrows as one gets closer to the origin.

FOR
ALLAH

KHALQ (Creation)

ZONE OF EXISTENCE & CREATED
WORLD

WORLD OF OPPOSITES/CONFLICTS
& DUALITY

TRANSIENT WORLD OF TURMOIL &
CONSTANT CHANGE

The journey of the Seeker

(from Creation to Creator & back without return)

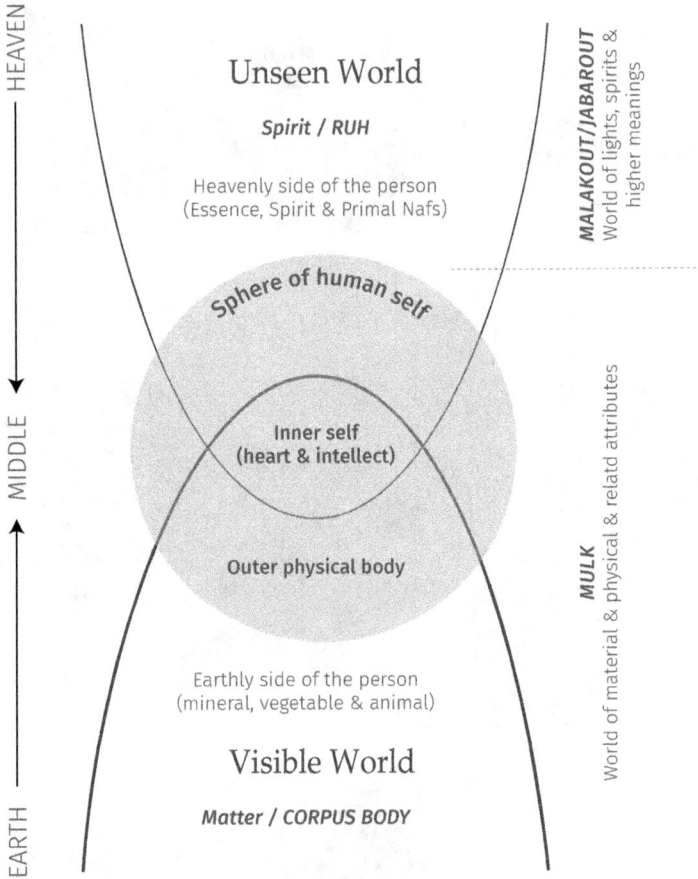

Unseen World

Spirit / RUH

Heavenly side of the person
(Essence, Spirit & Primal Nafs)

Sphere of human self

**Inner self
(heart & intellect)**

Outer physical body

Earthly side of the person
(mineral, vegetable & animal)

Visible World

Matter / CORPUS BODY

HEAVEN

MIDDLE

EARTH

MALAKOUT/JABAROUT
World of lights, spirits &
higher meanings

MULK
World of material & physical & relatd attributes

*The lights & designs activates matter to produce the interspace
between the high & low, between the finite & infinite, the human self
(nafs). The nafs arises when the spirit from the unseen world brings life
to the body and soul of the material world.*

Journey of Self

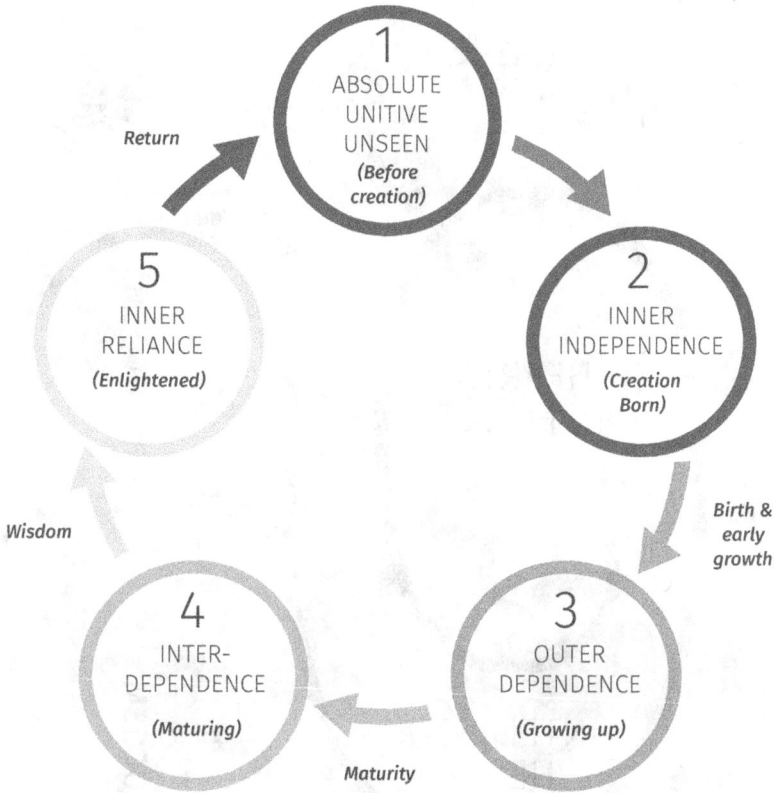

1
ABSOLUTE
UNITIVE
UNSEEN
(Before creation)

2
INNER
INDEPENDENCE
(Creation Born)

3
OUTER
DEPENDENCE
(Growing up)

4
INTER-
DEPENDENCE
(Maturing)

5
INNER
RELIANCE
(Enlightened)

Return

Birth & early growth

Maturity

Wisdom

A

Process of Human Emanation & Evolvement

- Zone of lights & spirits
- Primal designs & patterns of energies

HIGHER COSM
JABAROUT

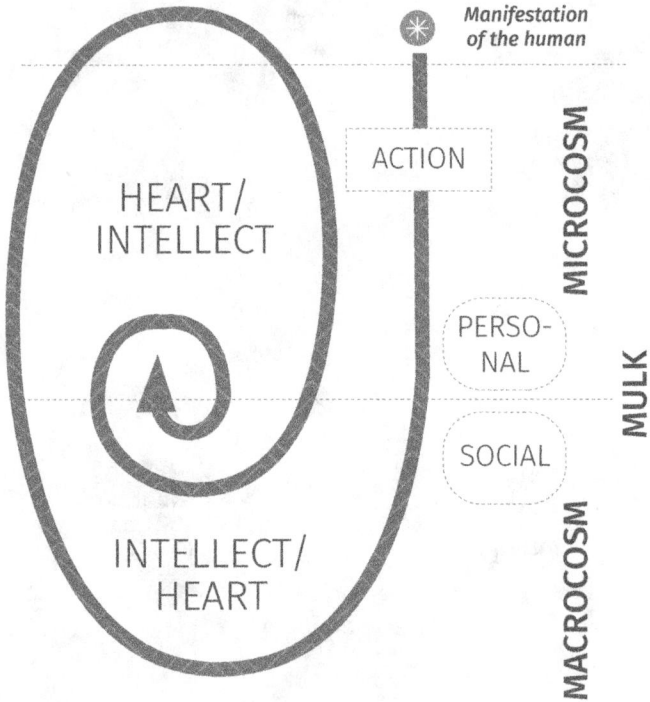

Manifestation of the human

ACTION

MICROCOSM

HEART/
INTELLECT

PERSO-
NAL

MULK

SOCIAL

INTELLECT/
HEART

MACROCOSM

B

C

Essence   (DIVINE
                          REALITIES)

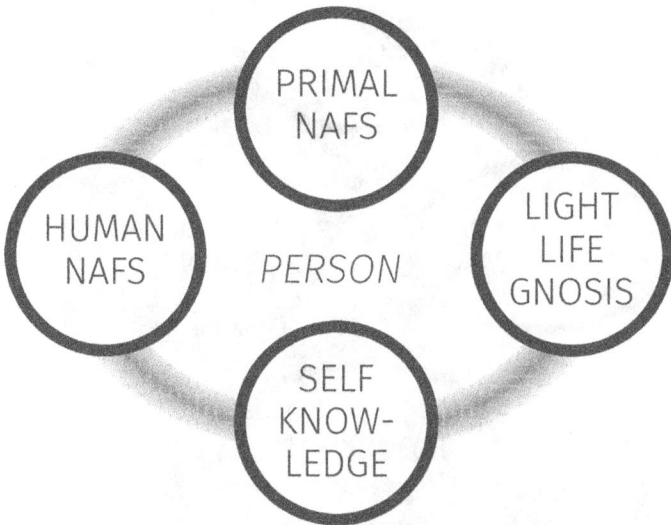

Form   (EXISTENTIAL
                         REALITIES)

D

ATTRIBUTES
DHIKR &
AWARENESS

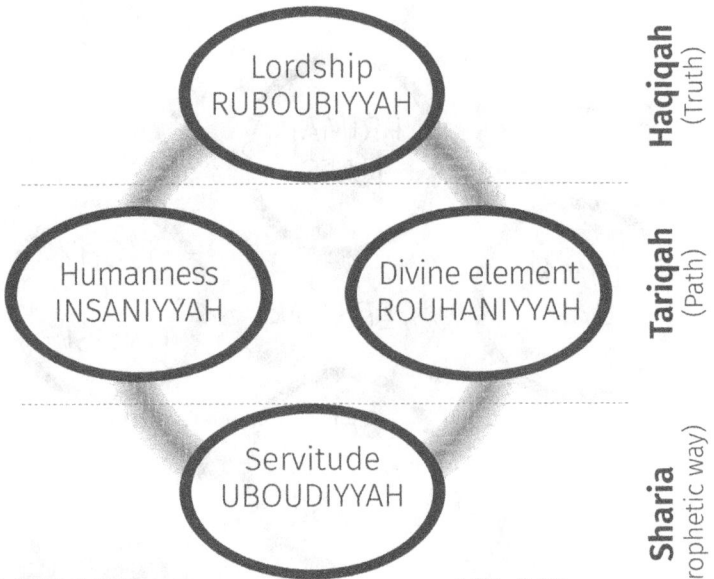

Lordship
RUBOUBIYYAH

Haqiqah
(Truth)

Humanness
INSANIYYAH

Divine element
ROUHANIYYAH

Tariqah
(Path)

Servitude
UBOUDIYYAH

Sharia
(Prophetic way)

ACTIONS
SERVICE &
COURTESY

**-ISLAM
-IMAN
-IHSAN**

Prophetic Attributes

JABAROUT
Pre-existence Zone
(Pure essence)

MALAKOUT
Primal Creational Zone

Manifestation of primal lights
& designs zone of spirits

RUH
FITRAH
(Primal Nafs)

Rabb/Abd
Ruh/Primal Nafs

BY MEANS OF

BY MEANS OF

Body/Limbs Mineral Veg.Animal	**INSANIYYAH** (Humanness) **NAFS** (Self)		**ROUHANIYYAH** (Spirituality) **RUH** (Spirit)	NUR (Light) Life
Five inner senses	**AQL / FIKR** (Intellect & Cognition) Thinking & Reflection	WITNESS MONITOR RECORD/ COMPANION	**QALB** (Heart) Insight & Inspiration	MARIFAH (Gnosis)
Search Applied Din +Knowledge	**ILM /FIQH** Knowledge Deep understanding		**DHIKR** (Rememberance & Awareness) path of Faith & Commitment	Discipline Service Constancy Patience

MULK (Manifested realities)

ACCEPTING &
DEVELOPING THE
PRIMAL CODE

SELF DEVELOPMENT &
KNOWLEDGE OF NAFS

To harness: primal drives
biological drives
psychological drives

JABAROUT: *Essence, Root, Divine Command*
MALAKOUT: *Spirits, Lights, Designs & Patterns*
MULK: *Existential Manifestations, The world of manifested realities.*

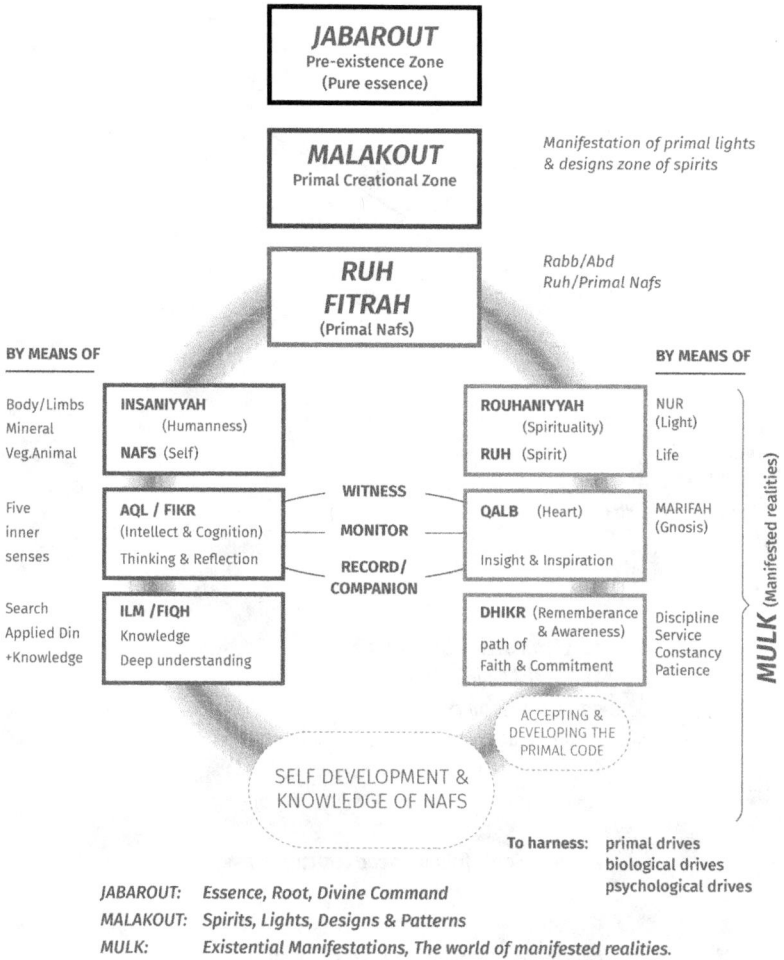

Basic Sketch of
Cosmology of
Spirit/Soul/Self & Heart

LIGHT FROM THE SPIRIT

A

UNSEEN
or non material
world

B

Physical World

Man is composed of:
Spirit
Heart
Mind/Intellect
Self/Soul (including body)

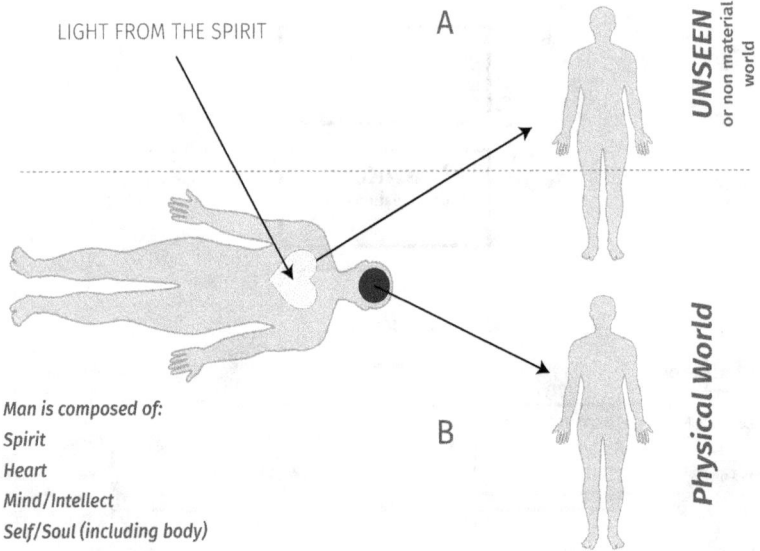

A. Person acting through heart:
This is the "middle path". Head above
earth & feet on earth.

If heart dominates above head, then the resultant
action produces a beingness that encompasses the
seen & unseen. One is the world but not of the world

B. Person only follows head (calculation &
reason)

If emotion emanates only from the head (i.e. reason &
rationality) the resultant being is only earthly. No
exposure to the unseen zone of light & the unseen
world.

Living through heart/head
or head only

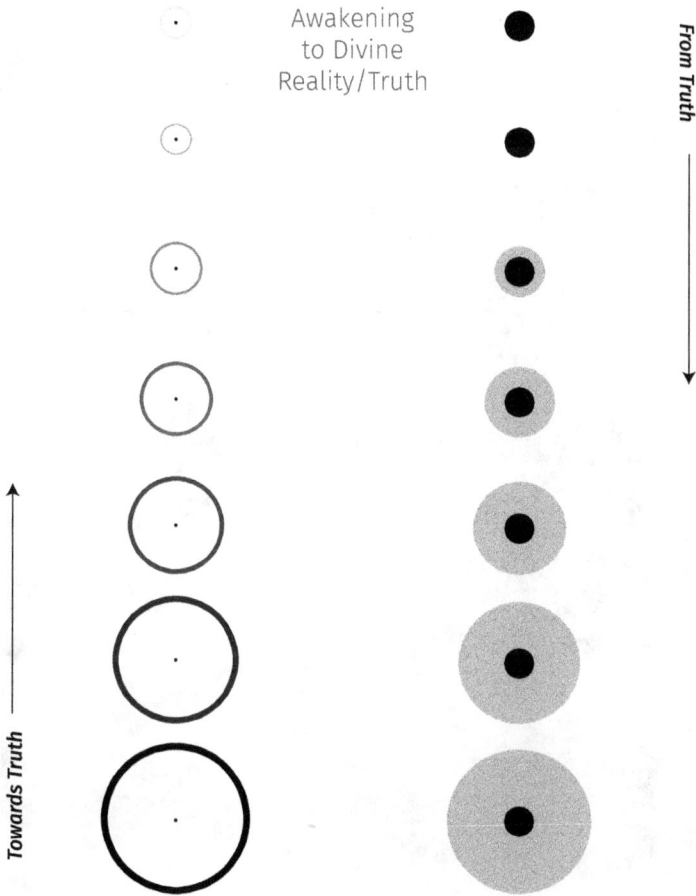

Awakening
to Divine
Reality/Truth

From Truth

Towards Truth

As you see yourself by
your Nafs
(vanishing outer self)

As you see yourself by
by the divine essence
in you (Ruh)
(accepting the outer self)

You do not see other than what you see